# LIMITED BY BODY HABITUS:
# AN AMERICAN FAT STORY

# LIMITED BY BODY HABITUS

## AN AMERICAN FAT STORY

JENNIFER RENEE BLEVINS

AUTUMN
HOUSE PRESS

Pittsburgh

**ISBN: 978-1-938769-40-5**

**LCCN: 2019933584**

www.autumnhouse.org

Autumn House Press receives state arts funding support through a grant from the Pennsylvania Council on the Arts, a state agency funded by the Commonwealth of Pennsylvania, and the National Endowment for the Arts, a federal agency.

*For my family*

*fat*

*overweight, obese, morbidly obese*

*underheight, obeast, ginormous*

*generously proportioned, gravitationally challenged, fluffy*

*roly-poly, jelly-belly, potbellied*

*hefty, husky, chubby, chunky, beefy, bulky, porky, portly, pudgy, paunchy, shapely, fleshy, sturdy, stocky, lardy, lumpy, dumpy, weighty*

*plus-sized, queen-sized, big girl, big-boned, larger woman, full-figured, matronly, curvy, curvaceous, corpulent, voluptuous, Rubenesque, zaftig, BBW*

*plentiful, ample, rotund, robust, solid, stout, round, plump, thick*

*meaty, meat on their bones, more cushion for the pushin'*

*well-fed, well-built, heavyset, filled out, overstuffed, upholstered*

*pig, sow, heifer, cow, porcine, bovine, whale, elephant, whelaphant, butterball*

*inflated, blimp; an inflated blimp*

*large, huge, immense, enormous, massive, gargantuan, colossal*

*unwieldy, disgusting, gross, lazy, lazy asshole, fat bitch, fat asshole, fat-ass, lard-ass, fat-so, fat chick, fatty, fatty-fatty-two-by-four-can't-get-through-the-kitchen-door*

*fat*

# Preface

YOU FEAR THE obesity epidemic because you've been told that fat is a lethal disease spreading like a contagion across the country. You stay away from fat (and fat people) because...well, you don't know why. It is an epidemic, after all. You could catch it. You could catch The Fat. It could disperse—it could leak through the boundaries of other bodies and spill into your own. Yes, I understand. Fat is terrifying.

My mother and grandmother taught me to cut the fat off of every piece of meat I eat. Granny would use special meat scissors to slice the pearly white chunks of fat off of chicken cutlets and steaks before preparing them for the oven. Fat is not good to eat, I was taught.

I was also taught that it's not good to be fat. I should want as little fat on my body as possible, I was told. I used to imagine using Granny's special meat scissors to slice fat off of my thighs, arms, stomach.

According to a 2011 study, some Americans would rather be blind, lose a limb, or give up five years of their lives than be obese.

Granny and my mother encouraged me to befriend girls who were heavier so I would be perceived as skinny in comparison. Proximity to fat, in their estimation, would somehow negate my own. If this were true, then airline passengers wouldn't complain about being seated next to a fat person. Commuters wouldn't give fat passengers on subway cars dirty looks. Fat kids wouldn't eat alone at lunchtime.

In the moment that I type this sentence, I am not fat; by the time you read it, however, I might be fat. You might be fat someday, too. Or someone you love might get fat. And that person you love—a partner, a friend, a parent—might one day decide to let a surgeon chop up their insides with meat scissors because they don't want to be fat anymore. Because their doctors told them that their fat would kill them. Because they couldn't get hired, or get a date, or order a meal in public without being judged, mocked, or given unsolicited health advice.

And that surgery could go wrong—so wrong that you suddenly find yourself standing beside their hospital bed, suctioning the phlegm leaking out of the tracheostomy hole in their neck, bearing daily witness to the disaster that has become their life. And you start hating fat even more than you did before the surgery because you blame everything on the fat, when really it was the meat scissors. It was the surgery that promised thinness. The culture that taught you to fear fat more than death. The society that convinced you that technological wonders like weight loss surgery trump natural design.

And as you tend to your loved one's fat, battered body and try to comfort their delirious, rattled mind, you notice your own body and mind changing. Months of sitting vigil have enlarged your thighs. Countless encounters with the fat prejudice of the medical industry have expanded your mind. You begin to see connections and patterns between your disaster and another disaster happening hundreds of miles away. You start to think that maybe you were right—maybe we do leak into other bodies. Maybe the boundaries between us are malleable, mercurial, soft.

You spend a summer watching spillage, and it changes you.

Sometimes I worry that I have waited too long to write about the summer of 2010. At the time, the stakes were so high and the circumstances so absurd that it was as if I were living inside a movie about my life, not my actual life. I don't know if I will ever feel that same sense of endorphin-stimulated urgency again. As the disaster unfolded, my feelings about what was happening and who had wronged me were crystallized, absolute, inconvertible. I was righteous indignation incarnate, and my mission was clear: save my father and, in doing so, save my family.

But sometimes I worry that I haven't waited long enough to write about that summer. I am concerned that my account of the disaster will piss off the living and disrespect the dead. I'm now somewhat ashamed of the Jennifer who saw the situation so clearly—the me who thought that it's possible to save the people we love, the me who thought it was all about her. My father's gastric bypass experience (and the years of research and writing about it that I have done since) completely changed how I feel about fat, bodies, love, and death. And since those feelings keep evolving and changing, I worry that I'm not yet enlightened enough to write this story.

And I'm afraid to write about fat. I worry that I'll piss off skinny people who believe that fat is inherently unhealthy, and fat people who believe that fat is never unhealthy. And even just using the word "fat" may piss people off, but medical terms like "over-weight," "obese," and "morbidly obese" pathologize fatness, implying that fatness is a disease, which I don't necessarily believe. Well, at least not anymore.

I don't know how to write about fat, and I don't know how to tell this story. So I'll just begin here:

On the morning of March 24, 2010, my father walked into a hospital in Durham, North Carolina for a routine gastric bypass procedure. My mother and I walked in with him.

# SECTION ONE:

# Reports a Long History of Obesity

OPERATIVE REPORT

DATE OF SURGERY: 03/24/2010

INDICATION: This is a 61-year-old white male with a body mass
index of 50 who has failed at previous medical weight loss
attempts, who has undergone our comprehensive preoperative
bariatric evaluation, has attended educational classes,
and underwent a 1 hour consent group class where risks and
benefits of gastric bypass were explained in detail and where
all questions were answered. On the morning of the surgery,
it was confirmed that the patient remained aware of the risks
and benefits of surgery, was aware that this was an elective
procedure, and wished to proceed with surgery.

# RYBG—Surgery #1

## NORTH CAROLINA, MARCH 2010

WE STOPPED AT a Starbucks drive-thru. I ordered coffee, my mother ordered a piece of lemon pound cake and a strawberry smoothie, and my father ordered nothing. I drove, my mother sat beside me, and my father sat in the backseat. He started getting anxious on the interstate. My mother commanded him to "Breathe, Jim! Breathe! Calm down and breathe!" I judged her harshly for that piece of lemon pound cake, which I now regret, which is unfair. Regret undoes nothing, and, at the time, I was angry with both of them for getting so goddamn fat. Just as she had every right to exist in that moment, be fat, and eat a piece of pound cake, I had every right to resent her existence, fatness, and choice of breakfast food. Now that those things are no longer true (i.e., her existence, my resentment), it's very tempting to judge myself harshly for the things I said and felt back when they were true.

The three of us sat together in pre-op behind a blue and green checkered curtain. I was in a green shirt, my mother was in a red shirt, my father was in a hospital gown. My mother was wearing her gold hoop earrings. I wore no jewelry. When I was growing up, she used to get annoyed when I would leave the house with no jewelry on. She would crinkle her nose and make her smelling-shit face. "You look so much better with jewelry," she would say.

People came in and out of our little enclosure. A nurse. An anesthesiologist. The surgeon, Dr. Belfore.[1] In the picture a nurse took of us in pre-op that morning, I'm sitting on the gurney next to my father, and my mother sits to my other side in a chair. My father and I are leaning in toward each other, grinning optimistically. My mother sits slightly apart from us with a pleasant but neutral expression on her face.

When I look at that picture now, I understand that the not-a-smile, not-a-frown on my mother's face is a mask that punishes us both. It simultaneously conveys and suppresses her jealousy of my youth/my body/my freedom/my father's affection for me. At the same time, it walls up her delicate, obsessive heart, which contains love for us too scary, too primal for her to feel. The expression on her face performs an aesthetic function as

---

[1] Name has been changed.

4

well. My mother rarely smiled in pictures toward the end of her life; she avoided being photographed as a general rule because of her weight. Smiling makes one's face look fatter. I know this because, as a pudgy adolescent, I spent hours in front of my bedroom mirror practicing how to smile without making my face look bigger; when I was successful, the resemblance to my mother was uncanny.

Dr. Belfore used a purple marker to draw the letters "RYGB" (Roux-en-y/Gastric Bypass) on my father's belly. Underneath she wrote her initials and drew a smiley face. A placard on the wall above my father read, "We strive to provide excellent care. If we have not met your expectations, please let us know."

I snapped a picture as orderlies in blue caps wheeled my father off to surgery. In the photo, his arms are crossed atop his belly and he smiles tentatively. My mother and I were given a pager that looked like the kind you get at a place like Applebee's when you're waiting for a table. We took it with us down to the basement cafeteria, where we went to eat and wait.

# When Diet and Exercise Just Aren't Enough

GASTRIC BYPASS, OR Roux-en-Y, is currently considered the "gold standard" of surgical weight-loss procedures. I knew very little about gastric bypass when our disaster started; now I know that gastric bypass, typically performed laparoscopically, reduces the size of the stomach by 90 percent. Surgeons cut away part of the upper stomach and create a new stomach pouch that can hold only 15 to 30 cubic centimeters at a time—about the size of an egg. Then they bring a tube up from the small intestine and connect it to the new stomach pouch. The rest of the old stomach (now called the "remnant stomach") remains connected to the small intestine and continues to aid in digestion. The remnant stomach never ingests food again, so it just floats in the body like a ghost ship. When successful, it is generally believed that gastric bypass serves as an impressive example of the medical industry's ability to cure the "disease" of obesity, while also resolving some medical issues believed to be caused by obesity, such as sleep apnea, type 2 diabetes, and high blood pressure. When unsuccessful, gastric bypass can cause internal bleeding, bowel obstruction, infection, pulmonary embolism, and death. Even though the potential consequences of gastric bypass are so extreme, fat patients (for instance, both of my parents) are frequently encouraged by their physicians to get the surgery because they claim that the benefits offset the risks.

The quest to "cure" obesity has become quite a booming business. Ever since Surgeon General C. Everett Koop launched a campaign against fat in the mid-1990s, obesity has been perceived as "a public health issue that is among the most burdensome faced by the Nation." Capitalizing on the pervasive fat hatred that has persisted in the US since the Industrial Revolution, the medical community, drug companies, and the government have worked tirelessly over the last twenty-five years to convince us that if we allow our body weight to exceed the limits of the "normal" range of an arbitrary measurement of health (i.e., Body Mass Index, or BMI), then we are contributing to a massive public health epidemic. Thanks to the success of this anti-fat campaign, the American Medical Association, Medicaid, and Medicare currently classify obesity as a disease. As a result of this classification, most insurance plans now cover weight loss surgery. My father's gastric bypass surgery, for instance, was covered by his insurance.

BMI is the primary diagnostic tool used by doctors and insurance companies to determine a patient's eligibility for bariatric surgery, even though numerous medical experts have contended that it is a poor indicator of health. In 1998, the National Institutes of Health lowered BMI levels—a change that made millions of Americans "overweight" or "obese" literally overnight (and which coincided neatly with the commencement of the media onslaught about the "obesity epidemic"). The International Obesity Task Force, the committee largely responsible for the World Health Organization (WHO) report that influenced this BMI change, had direct financial ties to pharmaceutical companies that manufactured diet pills for profit. Currently, approximately 228,000 weight loss surgeries are performed each year in the US at a cost of $15,000 to $25,000 per surgery. In 2018, the total value of the US weight loss market was $72 billion. So far, the war on fat has been a highly ambitious and lucrative endeavor.

# We Tell Ourselves Stories in Order to Live

NORTH CAROLINA, MARCH 2010

My MOTHER AND I took the pager with us to the hospital's cafeteria. We filled our trays with food, paid the cashier, and sat down at a table. I had planned for this moment—the moment when the waiting would begin and I would be alone with my anxious and worried mother. Typically, my mother and I could only spend an hour or two alone together before we would start to fight (we could last a little longer if other people were present), so I had been nervous about passing this time together ever since my father had announced his decision to get gastric bypass.

My plan was to keep my mother talking about other things. Her default mode tended to be hyperbolic-catastrophic: "The sky is falling. The world is ending. Your father is going to die and then what's going to happen to me. Our lives are over. Your life is over. No man is going to want you with your hair dyed that color." And so on.

She liked that mode. "I like to worry," she would tell me. "I enjoy it." And she meant it—I could tell by the supreme satisfaction she garnered from imagining all of the horrors that might befall her and those she loved. The only activity she seemed to enjoy more than worrying about hypothetical, apocalyptic future scenarios was to rehash family lore. Like the oral storytellers of ancient cultures, my mother and grandmother passed down family legends through colorful tales of injustice, ingratitude, and inequity. I grew up listening to their monologues about the cherry pie that killed my great-great-grandmother in Italy. The caustic feud over the inscription on (and ownership of) a gravestone in a cemetery in Queens that cost $625 during the Great Depression. The little bitch who betrayed Granny on the day of her eighth-grade graduation. The two of them would get so fired up—sometimes working themselves into a frenzy—as they sat at the kitchen table together, drinking hot tea and eating Entenmann's crumb coffee cake, retelling the stories of the tragedies and injustices that they and our ancestors had endured. It was an art, really. Sometimes I miss it.

So my plan for the hours I would spend waiting with my mother during the surgery was to have her repeat the greatest hits of our family lore while I transcribed her stories onto my laptop. I figured it would be the best way to keep her mind from defaulting to hyperbolic-catastrophic mode. Also, I genuinely wanted to preserve the stories. I hated having to listen to them over and over again as a kid, but I had become hungry for them as an adult. I had started seeing them as a potential roadmap—a guide for avoiding the same pitfalls and mistakes in my own life. Also, I found them totally fascinating and occasionally bizarre.

The pager sat between us on the table, amidst empty wrappers and half-eaten food. As she talked and I transcribed, my mother picked at the leftover food. There was one story in particular that I wanted her to retell, given the events that were unfolding that day. She didn't bring it up on her own, so I decided to ask: "Who was the one who had to be lifted out of her house by a crane after she died?"

"Elizabeth Correll," she said. "Very sad story." She told me that the Corrells lived on the east side of Manhattan, but eventually bought a house in Jackson Heights, Queens (where my mother was born and raised). Elizabeth had four children, one of whom was my great-grandfather, Fred. Her only daughter, Eliza, died at the age of fifteen from tuberculosis. Depressed from the loss of her daughter, Elizabeth gave up—stopped moving, stopped living. "She had everyone waiting on her," my mother told me. As a result, she weighed over 300 pounds when she died. "They had to put her in a piano crate and use a crane to lower her body out of the building because they couldn't take her down the stairs," my mother said.

I wanted her to see parallels between our present-day circumstances and those of our ancestors, which is why I had asked her to retell that story. But either she didn't notice them, or they were too painful to acknowledge, because she immediately moved on to the story about her Italian great-uncle losing his fingers while making paint for the Patterson-Sargent Company.

I felt like I had been watching my mother gradually turn into Elizabeth Correll. When I was growing up, my mother was beautiful, powerful, and terrifying. She cared for us with an obsessive fervor; my brother and I knew we were loved, and that love scared the shit out of us. But after Granny died in 2003, my mother decided that she wasn't going to take care of anyone anymore, including herself.

She detached from the world—few friends, no outside activities. She even stopped driving. The fiery glory of her bipolar disorder extinguished by medication and age, and her thinning gray hair turned completely white, she now spent most of her days in her pink recliner, covered by a blanket and a cat or two, sleeping or watching television.

Her weight had fluctuated up and down as I was growing up, but during the last seven years she had gained so much weight that she had started having difficulty walking even very short distances. She didn't monitor her blood sugar or care for her type 2 diabetes consistently. Eating seemed to be one of her few sources of happiness.

I don't think her decline was due to depression after losing a loved one, as was (allegedly) the case for Elizabeth Correll. Her perpetual, toxic quarrel with Granny (about everything and nothing) had kept her sharp and fired up, and caring for Granny in her final years had given her a focus and purpose after Ray and I left home. Granny's death devastated her, but more than anything I think it allowed her to fully unleash the sadness that had been simmering beneath her surface for most of her life. In the stories she told me of her childhood, she often painted a grim picture of a lonely little fat girl who longed for the father and brother I had but that she had been denied (Granny had a boy who died during childbirth in the late 1930s, and my grandfather died when my mother was a baby).

But I know that there had been times when she had been happy. Granny, too. They would deny it, of course, but I saw it with my own eyes. I saw that my father made them both happy. His nickname for Granny was "Wub," which was derived from a silly, nonsense name that Granny and my great-aunts used to call each other—"Wubba" or "Wubbakaduzza"; my father didn't feel comfortable calling her "Helen" or "Mom," so he called her "Wub" instead. They shared a love for quality coffee and my mother. He would often soften the tension during a fight between Granny and my mother (later, between my mother and me) by interjecting some smart-ass remark or simply changing the subject. My father was the mediator, the balancer, the voice of reason.

As my mother finished retelling me the gravestone-purchase-during-the-Depression story, we were interrupted by a young male nurse who was, as Granny would say, a "good lookin' fella." He introduced himself, asked how we were doing and why we were in the hospital that day, and then offered to take our trays for us. My mother and I looked at each other and exchanged a quick smile while he flirted with me. As we walked back to the elevator, we discussed whether or not a hospital cafeteria is an appropriate place to flirt with strangers. "Well, at least he was good lookin'," she said, "and has good taste. Shame he wasn't a doctor, though."

# A Note Regarding Writing About My Mother

I DON'T KNOW how to write about my mother.

But I can't *not* write about her, because she is an integral part of this story.

She wanted me to call her Mommy, not Mom. After I reached a certain age, calling her Mommy made me feel like a baby, but she would get hurt and upset when I called her Mom, so I gave her what she wanted. When I write about her I tend to call her "my mother," because to call her "Mom" feels like a lie, and calling her "Mommy" confuses people who don't understand why a grown woman would call her mother "Mommy." Interestingly, it has never felt odd to call my father "Daddy," even in adulthood. I've been told that may be a "Southern thing," but I think it's something more than that. Perhaps it's because he never commanded me to call him anything at all.

It's like I can't really see her. Not accurately. She hovers an inch beyond the scope of my peripheral vision. I can feel her there, judging and loving me, but I can't see her. When she was alive, she probably couldn't see me, either; I look too much like her.

I started keeping a diary when I was six years old. It was my mother's idea. She bought me a little square-shaped, pink Cabbage Patch Kids diary and told me I should start writing in it because I would enjoy reading it one day. When I told her that I didn't know what to write, she suggested that I just write down what I did each day.

My first entry:

10/5/85

*Today I Watched*
*Cartoons and Went to*
*Hanes Mall. I got tie*
*shoes and This Diary*
*I didn't go to School. I*
*Tried to Call Shonda and Angela L. and Lacy. I*

*Talked to Lacy, [my] Good Friend*
*I don't go to School on*
*Sunday. This was a Nice*
*Day. I Love my Mommie*
*a Lot and She Loves me*
*too. My Family is nice. My*
*daddy make's money for us.*
*I like this Diary oh Yes.*
*I guss it is time to go*
*bye-bye*

I remember lying in front of the television on the beige carpet in our living room and composing my inaugural entry, surrounded by my family. I presented it to my mother when I was done. The bracketed "my" floats above the word "Good"—a correction in my mother's handwriting.

In this entry, six-year-old Jennie reveals her perception of the gendered division of labor in the family: Mommie administered love, daddy paid our bills. I am able to trace the evolution of my relationships with my parents through diary entries. Between ages six and ten, my allegiance and affection lay firmly with my mother. At age ten-and-a-half, I started paying attention to my father:

*4/30/89*

*Today nothing really happened. I can't wait to see Andy. Daddy and I went to Uptons to exchange the watch we got Granny because it was too small. Then we went to "Waldon Books" and I got 5 books. Daddy and I really haven't been that close for a while. I wonder why?*

Around age eleven, I began rejecting my mother:

*3/16/90*

*Remember I used to hate my father? Well, that's changed. I hate my mother now way more than I hate my father!! She drives me crazy!!*

Journal entries from my mid- to late-twenties indicate that my allegiance and affection eventually transitioned to my father. By the time I found myself riding in an ambulance with him to an ICU in Durham at the age of thirty-one, I considered him to be one of my best friends.

In *The Reproduction of Mothering*, Nancy J. Chodorow posits that a daughter's inevitable, Oedipal turn to her father is "both an attack on her mother and an expression of love for her."

As I write this, I am thirty-eight years old and have been keeping a journal for thirty-two years. Perhaps this is also an expression of love for her.

# In Which I Train Myself How to Detach

NORTH CAROLINA, 1985

I AM ABOUT six years old the night I start hating my body. On the way home from dance class, my mother tells me that I should want to look like Elizabeth. Elizabeth is a girl in my dance class who is really skinny. I think Elizabeth looks like a horse, because she has a long face and big teeth. I really like my round face and it makes me sad to consider exchanging it for Elizabeth's horse face. But tonight I can't remember the word "face," so I ask my mother, "Can I keep my head and put it on Elizabeth's body?" She says no, I should want to look like Elizabeth. I am alone in the back seat of the car, looking through the window at the lights illuminating the houses we pass in the dark. I am very quiet as I try to figure out how to give my mother what she wants.

# When You Gotta Go, You Gotta Go

NORTH CAROLINA, MARCH 2010

I DON'T REMEMBER much about the events that transpired the afternoon after my father's first surgery. We were granted access to him in his room on the sixth floor in the bariatric wing of the hospital. I remember marveling at the size of the toilet in his bathroom. The toilet, along with everything else in his room, was specifically designed for "morbidly obese" patients. It was two to three times the size of a typical toilet, with curved metal handles on both sides. The handles looked a little like metal butterfly wings with holes carved out of the middle. I took pictures of the toilet. I felt like I was being indoctrinated into a whole new world—the world of really fat people. A place where "morbidly obese" was the new normal. Except it really wasn't, because all of the fat people were there because they were trying to get rid of their fat. So, in actuality, the bariatric wing of the hospital was a holding cell. A place where persons deemed unfit for society in their current form went to rehabilitate. To normalize. To shed their former selves—selves which could never be accepted in their current form. It was a false safe house. A ruse. The goal of bariatric medicine is to stop needing a Jacuzzi-sized, silver-winged toilet. To have an ass that fits appropriately into an airplane seat. To shrink. To disappear.

I vaguely recall that my father was drowsy and loopy after the surgery. He kept trying to keep his eyes open to interact with us, but his head would invariably fall back to the pillow. My mother slept in the recliner by his side that night. I was (and still am) moved by this gesture. It was one of the many instances I witnessed that year of my mother's obsessive love for and devotion to my father. Even though she had physically reached the point where she had difficulty just taking care of herself, and even though spending the night in a hospital room recliner (rather than her special, motorized recliner at home where she spent most of her time) would cause her considerable pain and annoyance, she still chose to stay. Probably because she felt that no one else could take care of my father like she could. She wanted to watch over him—to tell all of the medical personnel everything they were doing wrong. She believed that her presence there would protect him. I know all of this because I stepped into that same role about a week and a half later, and, once I did, I felt the same way.

She called me around six the next morning. Her voice was measured, but quivering with restrained volatility. She began by listing items she needed me to bring from home—primarily, a change of clothes for her. Then her voice buckled when she reached her thesis: My father had experienced some sort of heart attack. Or heart event. A stroke? She wasn't clear on this point. All I could discern was that something had happened earlier that morning that involved his heart, and they were going to take him back into surgery. She told me to get there as quickly as possible.

When I arrived about an hour later, she met me in the ICU waiting room. She was wearing nothing but my father's thin, blue robe that we had brought from home. She was crying, limping, falling apart at her seams. She was pushing a walker in front of her and looked to be on the verge of collapsing. She explained that she had been unable to get out of the recliner in the room the night before in time to make it to the bathroom when she had to pee, so she had peed all over herself, hence her need for a new set of clothes. I helped her into the bathroom and gave her the bag with her clothes.

After she changed, we sat together in the ICU waiting room. Rachel Ray was deconstructing a lasagna recipe on the television in the corner. A chaplain came and spoke with us, prayed with us. My mother cried. I can't remember if I cried. It's highly unlikely that I didn't.

When I saw her standing there, supported by a walker, wearing nothing but a thin, flimsy robe in public, I felt like a bad daughter. From my earliest days, I had been taught that it was my duty, my destiny to one day take care of my mother. Granny lived with us until she died, and her mother (Jennie D'Andrea—my namesake) had lived with her until she died, so according to the precedent that had been set in my family, in order to be a good daughter, I would one day have to live with my mother. I dreaded this fate. I lived in fear of the day when my father would no longer be able to take care of my mother and I would have to take over the job. That morning, I began to feel like that destiny was upon me.

I had seen my mother weak and frail, crying in various stages of undress before, but never in public like that. I felt like I had neglected part of myself—like *I* was the one standing there almost naked, covered in pee, barely able to stand up. She never would have let this happen to *me*, I thought. She would have taken care of *me*.

My brother Ray arrived mid-morning while our father was still in surgery. He was dressed in his police uniform. "I had to drive the patrol car down," he said. "I could get written up for that," he added. His eyes were red, bloodshot. He had been finishing up

16

the night shift when our mother called. At first he seemed annoyed when I told him that our father had not actually had a heart attack (which was the news he had heard from our mother). His annoyance eventually developed into relief, and I think he may have even been glad that he'd come. I could be wrong, though. You never can tell with Ray.

# The Brother She Never Had

RAY AND I both inherited the depression that runs on both sides of our family, but he seems to have received a double dose. Ray resents our parents for getting so goddamn fat, but he resents them even more for conceiving him. He has a lot of guns and a lot of anger, and he carries both around with him wherever he goes. He is now six feet tall and weighs about 280 pounds, but sometimes when I look in his face I am able to see the little boy I knew in the sad man he has become. He still has the same striking hazel eyes, the same long eyelashes that get caught in his glasses, and the same kindness that often made him the target of other kids' cruel jokes.

When we were little, Ray was both prophetically wise and heartbreakingly fragile. I was sixteen months older, so I assumed it was my duty to protect him. When I couldn't sleep, I would go into his room and watch him sleep. His dark brown hair would get wet with sweat and stick to his forehead. I loved his blue Transformer pajamas. I have a picture of him bursting out of those blue pajamas at the threshold of his fat stage, standing on his bed and pointing a toy gun at me. "I love him the most," I used to think as I stood over his sweaty, sleeping body. A few years later, I abandoned him. Once I entered middle school, I began avoiding our house and everyone in it. Ray, only ten years old at the time, confronted me one day when I wouldn't let him go bike riding with me. He said, "Pretty soon you'll go off to college and then we won't get to play together anymore." Thinking he was being overly dramatic, I hopped on my bike and pulled out of the driveway.

But as I grew older, I discovered that he had been right. Distancing myself from my family had also meant distancing myself from Ray, at a time when he really seemed to want me around. This consequence of my turn away from my family still breaks my heart.

When I was a child and my mother would explain why it had been so important to her for me to have the sibling-she-never-had, one reason she cited was that when I grew up, I would want to have someone in my life who knew what it had been like to grow up in our home. Once things went south after my father's gastric bypass, I could see what she meant. There were very few people who understood the complexities of our familial blueprint—who understood why our father's incapacitation was so very catastrophic for us. To most outside observers, he was just another sick father, another old fat man in a hospital bed, and our mother should be the one taking care of him. But Ray and I understood the difficult truth of the situation all too well.

# I Would Not Recommend My Program

MY FAMILY'S RELATIONSHIP to dieting was quintessentially American. Our lives were punctuated by Puritanical periods of deprivation followed by feeding frenzies. During my childhood in the 1980s, I watched the adults in my home engage in a series of crash diets that were always followed by bouts of maniacal consumption. By the time I reached adolescence in the early 1990s, I was well versed in the practice of yo-yo dieting.

My mother, father, and grandmother all dieted—sometimes as a group, sometimes individually. My father's diets were always motivated by necessity and usually the most dramatic of the family because, for decades, his weight was monitored by Uncle Sam.

Lieutenant Colonel Blevins was in the military for almost thirty years. After four years of active duty in Germany, he returned to the US to attend law school and subsequently served as a JAG (or, Judge Advocate General) officer. While I was growing up, he served in the National Guard and then finished his military career in the Army Reserves. In order to remain eligible for service, he had to stay below a certain weight; if he exceeded the weight limit, he would be placed on fatty probation, which required that he weigh in regularly rather than just once a year.

When my dad played football in high school, he was so skinny that he had to drink three milkshakes a day to keep his weight up. But by the time he reached middle age, the yearly weigh-in had become a problem. He would pack on pounds between weigh-ins, then scramble to lose them at the last minute. One year he cut it so close that he had to lose eight pounds in six hours. He took some diuretics and laxatives and bought a one-day membership to a gym on weigh-in day so he could sit in the sauna and steam room for hours, trying to shed pounds before the trip to the Reserves office. Believe it or not, he managed to pull it off. When I asked him once about the experience, he said, "I would not recommend my program. You won't see me doing late night TV commercials pushing my patented method."

I remember well the buildup to weigh-in day. About a month prior, he would start running around the neighborhood, listening to cassette tapes of Army drill cadences on his Walkman. Granny would stop cooking her delicious ziti and aromatic pot roast, and serve us tasteless boiled chicken and watery frozen vegetables instead. The entire family was on a diet by proxy. Granny became a diet despot, denying us all of the foods we loved and admonishing us when she caught us sneaking junk food. "What, so you wanna be fat, huh? What's amatta with you?!" she'd say when my mother, brother, and I would arrive home in the afternoon carrying McDonald's bags containing an "after-school snack."

"We're all too fat!" Granny would declare at random moments throughout my child-hood. She included herself in that assessment because, at the time, she was fat too. Well…pudgy, really. An adorable, pudgy Italian grandmother who stood about four feet, ten inches tall. Sometimes she would try to put us all on a diet even when it wasn't weigh-in month. Since she cooked our meals, we were at her mercy. It was impossible to hide from Granny. In addition to running the kitchen, she cleaned the house and did all of our laundry. She never left home unless she was going somewhere with us. I remember during one Granny-imposed diet period, I somehow managed to accrue a small collection of candy bars that I hid in my room. I foolishly shared this informa-tion with my father, who then shared it with my mother. One night my mother came into my room as I was sitting at my desk doing homework. "Daddy tells me you have chocolate," she said as she hovered over me in her baby blue robe. I had no choice but to surrender part of my stash.

From what my mother told me about her experiences growing up in Jackson Heights, her childhood and adolescence were one long Granny-imposed diet period. Everyone around my mother constantly told her that she was too fat and needed to lose weight. I remember one story she'd share about the asshole doctor who would tell her she was too fat every time she went to see him. She told me with pride about the day she finally stood up to him. She was in college by this point, I think, and one day he said some-thing about her weight that made her so mad she "told him off," walked out of his office, and never went back. In the photos from her college years that I've seen, she was both beautiful and thin. It's no wonder she had such a troubled relationship with her body.

My mother's most dramatic diet was Optifast. I think I was about nine or ten years old at the time, so I don't remember much about her experience. I do remember seeing Optifast shake packets all over the house, which came in vanilla, chocolate, strawberry, and orange cream. I also remember that my mother was even testier and shorter with me than usual, which makes sense—she was living on a diet comprised entirely of nasty-ass liquid "meal replacements." The Optifast website defines the program (which still exists) as "a medically-supervised weight-management program that closely monitors and assesses progress towards better health and emotional well-being," which sounds pleasant enough. But the name of the company reveals the truth behind their marketing euphemisms—the diet is a *fast* that is supposed to help fat people reach their "optimal" selves, I guess. I vaguely recall that my mother suddenly lost a lot of weight and then, almost as suddenly, gained it all back.

For the adults in my family, weight loss was about deprivation and self-loathing, and the ends always justified the means. Ray and I internalized and adopted these methods because we had no other guides. Both of us have experienced dramatic weight fluctuations since childhood. Ray's adolescent pudginess melted away by the time he graduated high school and entered the Army. When my mother and I picked him up from basic training at Fort Benning, he looked like a ghost of his former self. The bones in his temples were jutting out of his head. He gradually gained back some weight, but after his years of active duty were over he went through a period of such extreme weight loss that I was worried he might be anorexic. When I visited his apartment that year, the only food item his refrigerator contained was a bottle of ketchup.

As for me, I gradually started eating less and less as I reached my adolescent and teenage years. I didn't want to be so chubby, but the only way I knew how to lose weight was to imitate my parents' dieting habits and eat as little as possible. Sometimes Granny would say, "*Eat*, Jenn-i-fuh! You're gettin' so skinny! You eat like a bird!" Other times she would tell me I needed to stop eating so much because I was getting fat. She and my mother would sit at the kitchen table together and discuss all of my body's "problem areas" (almost always my thighs) when I walked by. When I started working out and lifting weights in high school, Granny frowned and wrinkled her brow when she noticed my developing arm muscles one day as I stood in the kitchen washing dishes. "What do you want to look like a man for, huh?! Don't you want a husband? What, you wanna be an OLD MAID?!"

I dieted throughout my teens and twenties. My methods included, but were not limited to, SlimFast, diet pills, Weight Watchers, the Atkins/low-carb diet, the grapefruit diet, and a (near) starvation diet. I was most successful on Weight Watchers, but I eventually gained back about half of the weight I had lost. And during the two or so years I was on it, I was unhealthily obsessed with every little morsel of food or drink that passed my lips. I could think of little else but the "points" that I consumed each day, the "activity points" I earned each day, and the "points" I had yet to consume. I even started a meditation practice during that period, in part to try to learn how to banish thoughts of food from my mind. I have a distinct memory of sitting on a meditation cushion in a zendo on 17th Street in New York City, trying to clear my mind of all thoughts—to let the thoughts "pass by like clouds" as the sensei had advised—but still doing my food math over and over again in my head, which usually went a little something like this: "I have one point left today, so I could eat an apple on the train on my way home. Or I could eat an apple on the train and a bowl of cereal when I get home, which means I would dip into my extra flex points for the week, which means I have to be really good tomorrow if I want to have enough points left to have a few drinks this weekend. Or I could go hungry tonight and end the day under my points limit, and then I might actually lose some weight this week. But will I be able to sleep tonight if I'm this hungry?" And so on.

None of our diets worked, at least not long-term. As a family, we have collectively lost and regained hundreds of pounds over the years—our bodies contracting and expanding like balloons in the process. My body bears the marks of repeated weight loss and gain; I have subtle stretch marks on my upper arms, lower abdomen, and thighs. I imagine that the stretch marks on the bodies of my other family members are less subtle. Our bodies remember what we do to them. We are walking chronicles of both kindness and abuse, care and neglect.

But which is dieting? Kindness and care, or abuse and neglect? The 72-billion-dollar weight loss industry banks on us believing the former—that investing in their products is an investment in self-care, and that compulsive yo-yo dieting is better for you than "letting yourself go." From what I can tell, most doctors seem to agree that fat people should constantly strive to lose weight. Failing to lose weight on a diet—or losing weight and then gaining it back—is usually perceived as a failure of the dieter's will rather than of the diet itself.

This emphasis on losing weight is, of course, predicated on the belief that fat is inherently unhealthy. We've been told that too much excess fat on the body leads to all sorts of health problems, like high blood pressure, type 2 diabetes, sleep apnea, heart disease, depression, and cancer. In recent years, some researchers have been pushing back against the simple formula of "fat = bad" by presenting evidence that suggests body fat can actually be beneficial to your health. As Carl Lavie, cardiologist and author of *The Obesity Paradox*, puts it, "Fat isn't always bad. And exercise isn't always good." In his research, Lavie (and other physicians) have identified a "paradox" in regards to obesity: in a variety of illnesses—ranging from cardiovascular disease to kidney disease, cancer, arthritis, and HIV—patients who are overweight or slightly obese actually fare better than normal weight or underweight patients. Sandra Aamodt, a neuroscientist and author of *Why Diets Make Us Fat*, posits that it is possible to be fat *and* healthy because other indicators of good health, like blood pressure, cholesterol, blood sugar, and fitness level, are more important than (and not necessarily connected to) body weight. As Aamodt notes, "Low fitness, smoking, high blood pressure, low income and loneliness are all better predictors of early death than obesity." Researchers like Lavie and Aamodt argue that the emphasis should be on developing healthy eating and exercise habits rather than on losing weight through diets.

Perhaps the diet tide is beginning to turn. Numerous studies in recent years have produced evidence that suggests diets are ineffective, and even potentially harmful. In 2007, researchers who performed a comprehensive review of previous dieting studies concluded that "the benefits of dieting are simply too small and the potential harms of dieting are too large for it to be recommended as a safe and effective treatment for obesity." A 2016 study of former *The Biggest Loser* contestants found that they had regained about seventy percent of the weight they lost during the show and now burn about 500 calories a day *fewer* than other people their age and size; the crash dieting and brutal exercise regimen (and public fat shaming) they experienced on the show messed up their metabolisms and emotionally traumatized them. I even came across a study that suggests our weight is at least partially determined by our bodies' ability to process carbon dioxide—something that is completely beyond our control (until someone develops a carbon dioxide diet).

Weight loss surgery, such as the gastric bypass, gastric band, and gastric sleeve procedures, is modern medicine's answer to the dieting dilemma. This, of course, is where my family ended up. Decades of dieting culminated in an approach far more dangerous than Optifast, or laxatives and a sauna. My father went for broke—he chose to undergo the most aggressive, most "permanent" weight loss plan in existence.

I would not recommend his program.

# Without Evidence of Leak—Surgery #2

NORTH CAROLINA, MARCH 2010

DATE OF SURGERY: 03/25/2010

PREOPERATIVE DIAGNOSIS: Possible gastrointestinal leak

POSTOPERATIVE DIAGNOSIS: Old clotted intra-abdominal hematoma

CONDITION: The patient was extubated in the Operating room and transferred to the PACU in fair condition.

AFTER THE SECOND surgery was over, Dr. Belfore came out to the waiting room to update us. Her demeanor was casual, reassuring—she acted as if what had happened was no big deal. She said that there had been some old blood in his stomach, and they sucked it out. I don't remember much else about the exchange.

According to the medical records, he was taken into surgery because "[o]vernight, he had an episode of tachycardia into the 140's, complained of some more than usual abdominal pain, had a white count of 18, and evidence of a metabolic acidosis on blood gas. [The surgeons] therefore elected to take him to the Operating room as a Level 1, to rule out an enteric leak." The surgeons entered his abdomen through one of the laparoscopic "port sites" they had created during the initial surgery the day before and found "approximately 500 mL of old clotted blood," which they washed out with saline. The report reads, "The JJ [jejunal] was also carefully inspected and found to be without evidence of leak."

They let us see him briefly when they wheeled him out of surgery and into the hallway before taking him to the ICU. He was drowsy and drugged, but awake. He looked at us apologetically, as if he were sorry and somewhat ashamed to have caused everyone so much trouble, which made me so damn sad. It was the first moment of many that year that revealed to me a glimpse of who my father really was. This stripped-down, edge-of-life, helpless Jim Blevins was a new experience for me. I had only ever known him to be a quiet, sarcastic fortress.

My family had built our lives on the belief that my father was invincible. Soft-spoken, punctual, and profoundly capable, Jim Blevins was the most dependable person in my life. He never raised his voice, he was never late, and he never let me down. Over the years I watched as he salvaged remains from various disasters, both professional and personal, and still managed to take care of everyone he loved. It was very rare to witness any strong expressions of emotion from my father. His primary mode of communication was a deadpan sarcasm delivered as truth. Whenever I would misbehave as a little girl, he would threaten to give me to the gypsies so they could make fat baby soup out of me—"Just like we did to Siegfried and Brunhilda," my (fictional) older brother and sister, he'd say. The prospect of such an end frightened me. I was probably six or seven years old by the time I realized he was kidding (and much older by the time I realized his joke was kind of racist).

It was very difficult to discern what my father was really thinking or feeling. He once told me about a psychological evaluation he was given by one of his employers. When he met with the psychologist to discuss the results, he told him, "Mr. Blevins, you are an impenetrable box." My father told me this story with pride in his voice one night at the kitchen table as he played with his moustache, adjusted his eyeglasses, and stirred his drink with his finger.

It took quite a bit to penetrate that box; I know because I had a front row seat for its crumbling. The experience was like watching an imploded building fall in slow motion, the exterior partially retaining its form during the journey down.

# In Which I Train Myself How to Wake Up

COLUMBIA, SOUTH CAROLINA, 1997 & MY UNCONSCIOUS, 1985–1991

I'M HOME FOR the summer after finishing my freshman year of college. I go with my friends Kristin and Chad to check out a troupe of improv actors and psychologists act out audience members' dreams on stage. It's called "Dream Theatre," or something like that. They have props, costumes, and live musicians. Somebody heard that it's supposed to be pretty cool.

I sit with my friends in a small auditorium and watch as random audience members go up to the stage to stand in front of a microphone and tell their dreams, then have those dreams reimagined by a group of strangers. The actors use lots of brightly colored, flowing fabric. Wigs. Generic set pieces, like chairs and tables. The scenes are fantastical, funny, silly, absurd. A keyboard player improvises songs as the actors perform.

As I watch the troupe members run around the stage trailing long, flowing fabric and transforming the muck of someone's unconscious into a sort of reality, I consider getting up and sharing my dream. *The* dream. The nightmare I had every summer as a kid—sometimes before going to Grandmother and Pop-Pop's farm in the mountains of North Carolina for our annual summer visit, sometimes after. Sometimes both. Maybe it started in 1985, the summer after Uncle Craig killed himself. Maybe it started before. I'm not sure.

In the dream, I'm sitting in my grandparents' living room at dusk, surrounded by my family: Mommy, Daddy, Ray, Granny, Grandmother, Pop-Pop, Uncle Mike, and Aunt Onda. Sometimes even Uncle Craig is there. I am always very aware of the quality of the light. It's that time of day when there's still enough light outside to illuminate the inside of the house, but dark enough that the light in the house is hazy. That time right between day and night—right before someone reaches over and turns on a lamp.

As we sit quietly in a cluttered, musky room with matted shag carpeting and a working television stacked on top of an old, broken television, two gigantic trees in the front yard (dream trees, trees that didn't exist in real life) transform into colossal monsters, both at least fifty feet tall. I never get a good look at them, but I think they're like huge, gooey, hungry trolls. I'm the only one who notices them. "There are monsters in

27

the front yard!" I yell. At first, nobody believes me. I have to make my family see the monsters.

When the monsters begin to lumber toward the house, the rest of my family is frozen, petrified. I have to get them moving. I have to get us out of there. "We gotta get out of here!" I shout. They ask me what to do, where to go, how to escape. They all look to me to save them. I give them instructions: "The grandmothers can't run. We have to carry the grandmothers! We have to run!" I throw a grandmother on my back, my father throws the other grandmother over his shoulder, and I lead our retreat into the backyard.

My father always assists me, but in some versions of the nightmare I must first rescue him from the diamond mine in my grandparents' basement (dream diamond mine, dream basement). Two diamond-encrusted walls slowly begin to squish him (à la the trash compactor scene in *Star Wars*), and I have to pull him out before they succeed.

After I save my father and we throw the grandmothers on our backs, I lead us into the hills behind the house. When I believe we're far enough away, I instruct everyone to lie down in the tall grass and remain silent and still so the monsters won't find us. Less than fifteen feet away, they sniff and sort through the grass, searching for their lost meal. I always wake up right as the monsters get near.

At some point, I figured out how to wake myself up from the nightmare. Before going to sleep each night during the summer, I would sit up in my bed and memorize every detail of every item in my room. Stuffed animals. Cabbage Patch Kids. The mirror on the wall above my dresser. When I got older: the poster of Doogie Howser, M.D. on my wall. I would imprint the image of my room onto my brain and focus on it as I fell asleep. Then, when I found myself in that dimly lit living room facing those monsters, I would somehow make my conscious mind swoop in and bring me back to my bedroom. It didn't always work, but when it did I would wake up relieved and afraid, clutching my pink fuzzy blanket to my chest, and try to keep my eyes open until morning.

Now at eighteen, it's been years since I've had the dream. I'm convinced that the night-mare is over, so it might be cool to share it with a bunch of strangers and see what happens. It'll surely be the scariest dream that anyone shares tonight, so I wait until the end to volunteer because it's more dramatic to go at the end.

When they ask for one more dream, I raise my hand and they call me to the stage. In the heat of the spotlight, I tell everyone about the monsters. About my frozen, clueless family. About the light. The diamond encrusted walls. The grandmothers. The tall grass. I tell them how scary it always was. I don't tell them that memories of the dream still haunt me sometimes. I don't tell them about Uncle Craig.

I sit back down in the audience with Kristin and Chad as the actors gather together the necessary props and costume pieces. The accompanist plays a prelude while the actors assemble. Already I can tell that the music doesn't sound dark enough. It sounds almost mocking—like the guy at the keyboard is mocking my dream. It's cartoon dark, like on *Scooby-Doo* when Shaggy and Scooby get lost in a haunted mansion. It sounds stupid.

The actors start acting out the nightmare. Two of them stand on chairs and pretend to be trees that change into monsters, but they're not scary at all. They're not moving right. They're doing this swaying-back-and-forth thing with outstretched arms—like Frankenstein's monster or some generic boogeyman. People in the audience are laughing, and it's kind of pissing me off. The actors playing my family members are too fucking whiney, and the actor playing me isn't moving fast enough to get them out of there. Some douchebag keeps running back and forth across the stage trailing some douchey blue fabric. The audience roars with laughter during the grandmothers-on-the-back scene, and then all of a sudden it's over. Everyone claps, and I clap too because I'm supposed to. I agree with my friends that it was funny and cool, and then we go to a coffee shop to hang out.

But the performance wasn't funny, and it wasn't cool. The actors and the audience didn't get it. I threw Granny on my back and carried her into the hills because I love her and I didn't want the monsters to eat her. I rescued Daddy from the diamond mine because I was faster than everyone else and I knew what to do. I saved my family because nobody else could. Because they were all just standing there, waiting for someone to save them. Or waiting to die. I was never sure which.

# Master of My Fate

NORTH CAROLINA, MARCH 2010

AFTER THE SECOND surgery on Thursday morning, my father spent about a day and a half in the ICU. My mother stayed home on Friday to recover, Ray went back up to the mountains to return to work, and I spent the day in the ICU. To pass the time, I read my dad some of his literary favorites—"Invictus" (which William Ernest Henley composed in a hospital bed, making it a particularly fitting choice), "Jabberwocky," and the Saint Crispin's Day speech from *Henry V*. The surgeons wanted him to get out of bed and walk up and down the hall every few hours, which caused him a great deal of pain. So I tried to psych him up before every trip with some Henley: "It matters not how strait the gate, / How charged with punishments the scroll, / I am the master of my fate, / I am the captain of my soul." If that didn't work, I would drop some Shakespeare: "We would not die in that man's company / That fears his fellowship to die with us." He loves that shit.

Each trip down the hall was like going into battle. The nurses and aides would help him sit up on the side of the bed and then stand and grab onto a walker tall enough to have forearm rests. Then they would load up the walker with his oxygen tank, catheter bag, IV medications, and heart rate and oxygen monitor. Clad in only a hospital gown and blue sticky socks, he would slowly, laboriously push the walker and shuffle down the hallway of the ICU. I would walk beside him and tell him he was a badass.

Neither of us really had much frame of reference for how bad the recovery from gastric bypass was supposed to be, but so far it had been way worse than we had expected. In the mandatory informational sessions my father attended prior to the surgery, he had been told that he would be in and out of the hospital in "about three days" and able to return to work in a couple of weeks. Weight loss surgery had been presented to my parents as casual, relatively easy, and life-changing. They both planned on getting gastric bypass, but they decided that my father should go first because he was in better shape and had less weight to lose. So the idea was that he would have his casual, easy-breezy surgery, recover, and then take care of my mother later after she had hers. I would come down from New York for the week of his surgery, Ray would take off the following week to help with the recovery, and then life would slowly get back to normal. A trip to the ICU had never even been mentioned as a possibility.

He was in the ICU because they wanted to monitor his heart. As we would learn later (but which was not clearly communicated at the time), he developed atrial fibrillation after the first surgery—a heart condition that would remain an issue for quite some time. Even after he was transferred back to the bariatric floor on Friday night, he continued to have problems. The medical records confirm that he had nausea, vomiting, heart issues, and breathing problems throughout the weekend. The "surgery progress note" from the day after the second surgery says, "take back to OR (hematoma, ~~small leak~~)," and indicates that he was advanced to a "S2" or stage two diet, which meant that he could drink small amounts of Ensure in addition to drinking water. He kept complaining of pain. His walks down the hall became fewer and fewer because he said that it hurt too much to move.

Shortly before I left for the airport on Sunday, a surgeon I had not previously met came into the room. He admonished my father as if he were a bad child, threatening that he was going to develop pneumonia if he didn't get out of bed and walk. After the condescending lecture was complete, I left the room and walked down the hall to use the restroom. (I had stopped using the oversized bariatric toilet in my father's bathroom because sitting on it made me feel like Lily Tomlin in *The Incredible Shrinking Woman*.)

I started crying as soon as I closed the bathroom door. Every inch of me from my stomach to my brain knew that I should not get on my return flight to New York. I sensed that the situation was far more precarious than it appeared, and I worried that my mother and brother would have trouble dealing with any emergencies that might arise.

But I had just started a new job with an online publishing company about a month earlier, and I felt fortunate that they had given me the time off to come down to North Carolina for the surgery, even though I hadn't worked there long enough to accrue any vacation or sick time. I thought I had no choice but to return, even though the prospect of leaving made me want to vomit.

I ignored my body and returned to the room. I said goodbye to my parents, then Ray took me to the airport. I went back to work the following morning.

# Lifetime Member

NEW YORK, 2005

EVERY FRIDAY ON my lunch break, I walk five blocks to the nearest Weight Watchers meeting. I descend to a windowless, basement room and pay money to step on a scale and then sit in a plastic folding chair in the back of the room as I listen to strangers talk and joke and cry about food and fat. I rarely join the discussion. The meeting leader's favorite joke when asked questions about the point values of certain vegetables: "Listen people, nobody ever got fat by eatin' carrot sticks!"

I have lost twenty pounds in the last eight months. For the first time in my life, I am able to buy clothes in a size two. I am lithe. Light. Aerodynamic. The world has opened up and embraced me in new ways. A relative at Christmas: "Honey, you have A WAIST!" My (female) boss at the magazine where I work: "You're getting more gorgeous and glamorous with every pound you shed!" Random coworker: "Wow! You look SO much better!" I am constantly being applauded for taking up less space. I am learning that my old size twelve body was monstrous and unwieldy.

Today a young woman who looks to be about my age is crying. About a month ago she reached her goal weight—an impressive feat that we all applauded when the leader shared it with the group. But since then she's been gaining the weight back, and today her weigh-in was particularly demoralizing. In order to become "Lifetime Members," we have to remain within two pounds of our goal weight for at least six months, and then as long as we continue to maintain our weight, we can come to meetings for free for the rest of our lives.

The leader tries to console the young woman by putting her arm around her shoulder and nodding maternally. The crying woman says, "I just can't believe that I have to do this for the rest of my life. I can't believe that I have to be on a diet for the rest of my life."

DISCHARGE SUMMARY

DATE OF DISCHARGE: 03/29/2010

HISTORY OF PRESENT ILLNESS: Mr. Blevins is a 61 [year] old male who reports a long history of obesity. The patient's current body weight is 359 and height is 71, which leads to a calculated BMI )Body Mass Index) of 50. He reports the onset of weight gain approximately 10 years ago after he retired from the Army Reserve. He weighed approximately 240 pounds at that time. He gained weight gradually for approximately 5 years. Five years ago he fell and fractured his shoulder and then had knee surgery. His orthopedic issues led to a decreased activity level, and he gained additional unwanted weight. He states that he has very little dieting history, but feels that he is a good candidate for bariatric surgery. In addition the excessive weight aggravates management of the following co-morbid conditions: Benign Hypertension )401.1); Edema )782.3); Diabetes Mellitus )250); Mixed Hyperlipidemia )272.2); Sleep Apnea Nos )780.57); Backache Nos )724.5); Joint Pain-mult Jts )719.49); Depressive Disorder Nec )311)

FAMILY HISTORY: Patient indicates a family history of heart disease, arthritis, and early death.

SOCIAL HISTORY: Mr. Blevins is employed full-time as a Claims manager. He is married with 2 children. He is a former smoker from the ages of 18-40, 1 ppd. He is a social alchol [sic] drinker and denies the use of illegal substances.

# Goddamn Clusterfuck

NEW YORK, MARCH 2010

ONCE I RETURNED to New York after the initial gastric bypass surgery, my father's body started slowly shutting down. The problems started with a lump on the side of his face the day after he was discharged. Then the home healthcare nurse said that something was wrong with his heart. Then he was readmitted to the hospital, but he went to the local hospital in Burlington rather than the hospital in Durham where he received the surgery because he and my mother decided that Durham was too far away. The doctors at the Burlington hospital didn't seem to know how to care for a gastric bypass patient (a nurse there would later tell me that they didn't even have a CT scanner big enough to fit my father's abdomen).

Every day I received angry calls from my brother and bizarre calls from my mother. Ray's rage grew daily, and my mother couldn't comprehend that my father could be sicker than she was. "You know, I think whatever's wrong with your father's stomach is wrong with mine, too," she told me. Ray felt powerless, which made him furious. "They're all doing their own fucking thing, Jennifer. They won't listen to a word I say. It's a goddamn clusterfuck down here." My mother and brother sat in separate rooms in the same house, calling me at the same time, demanding sympathy and solutions. I wanted to give them both, but I couldn't really give them either.

On Thursday morning I called my father's hospital room from my office. He answered, and he was alone. "Oh thank God it's you," he said as soon as he heard my voice. "Everything's gone to shit down here." He sounded a little loopy, but I assumed it was just the result of pain medication. As we talked, I watched traffic move up Third Avenue. My father told me that I'm like titanium. "The strongest metal. That's you. You're my titanium."

I priced plane tickets on my office computer after we hung up. It was Easter weekend, so tickets were expensive. When I left to get my lunch, I rode the elevator down with Kathy, the office manager. I briefly told her about the situation and mentioned that I was considering flying down, even though I had just returned a few days ago.

"Well, if you rush down there now, then your family's going to expect that from you every time they have a problem. You need to take care of yourself, too," Kathy said.

As I sat in the Pret A Manger across the street from work and ate my spinach and goat cheese salad, I watched herds of New Yorkers power walk through the cool afternoon sun. I loved the anonymity, indifference, and impossibility of that place. New York City didn't give a shit about me, and she certainly didn't need me—two of the very reasons why I have always loved her so much. There I felt light and calloused, a free agent with a thick skin. I liked the Jennifer I was there.

When I returned to my office, I did not buy the plane ticket. I decided that they could figure this one out without me.

# SECTION TWO:

## An Unfortunate 61-Year-Old Gentleman

Patient Location: CRITICAL CARE UNIT CC16-1

DATE OF CONSULTATION: 04/04/2010

HISTORY OF PRESENT ILLNESS: The patient is a 61-year-old male who underwent recent bariatric surgery by Dr. Belfore at ———————— Hospital with a course notable for a take back with the finding of old hematoma in his peritoneal cavity as well as new onset atrial fibrillation who was transferred from ———————— Regional Hospital for further management of septic shock, acute renal failure, and hypoxia.

REVIEW OF SYSTEMS: The patient is currently in septic shock with a blood pressure of 60, and his review of systems is not obtainable.

# FLIGHT DL6559, LGA→RDU 04 APRIL 2010, 06:00 A.M.

IN THE SEAT next to the toilet, I sit and shake. Muscles clenched and freezing cold, I watch the sun come up through the oval-shaped window to my right. I can't control my convulsing because the synapses in my brain are blowing like fuses.

When the plane lands, I will run. First: car rental. Second: baggage claim. Third: speed a distance of sixty miles in a rental car to the hospital in Burlington. If stopped: Officer, my father is dying. First: car rental. Or first: baggage claim? Or car rental? *Is* my father dying?

A man exits the toilet and I can smell his shit. My muscles jump off of my bones. I am a jackhammer strapped to a seat. I am adrenaline and bile. I am the daughter, the sister. I am the one who left.

(*Fifteen hours earlier. JENNIFER on cell phone in lobby of Brooklyn movie theater.*)

MOTHER:      (*crying, uncharacteristically calm*) Your brother disappeared last night. I drove to the hospital today and had someone wheel me to your father's room in a wheelchair. I fell in his room and hit my face on the sink. I'm in the Emergency Room, and they're taking your father to the ICU.

(*JENNIFER on cell phone, walking out of Brooklyn movie theater.*)

FATHER:      (~~*crying*~~ *sobbing, disoriented, uncharacteristically desperate*) Oh God… Oh Jennie…help me…

(*JENNIFER on cell phone, running through streets of Brooklyn.*)

RAY:      (*screaming, characteristically angry*) <u>You're</u> the one who abandoned the family, goddammit! (*hangs up phone*)

# AN UNFORTUNATE 61-YEAR-OLD GENTLEMAN

At LaGuardia, the TSA workers patted me down and searched my bags. When you buy a plane ticket fifteen hours before a flight, you become a suspected terrorist. But I am white, female, and attractive, so the search and pat down were perfunctory. Pretty white girls don't blow up planes, apparently.

But I am not a girl on a plane. I am a soldier in a little boat in the opening scene of *Saving Private Ryan* and I am shaking so hard that my gun and teeth are rattling. We're about to storm the beach at Normandy and I just threw up in my helmet to be polite, but I should stop doing that. I should stop being polite. Because when this ship hits the beach, when that hatch falls open, I cannot be polite. I am Tom-fucking-Hanks and they're all depending on me and they're all holding their guts in their hands and crying for their mothers and begging me to save them or shoot them. I must save them or shoot them.

When this plane lands, I will run.

# Deus Ex Machina

NORTH CAROLINA, APRIL 2010

RAY MEETS ME in the hospital parking lot. It's bad, he says. Really bad. We strike a truce. I won't bring up the fact that he left on Friday night, he won't bring up the fact that I left years ago. We're scared, like little-kid scared. I want to hold his hand. I don't.

I talk to a nurse in the ICU and take notes: White blood cell count is forty-nine. Little to no urine output. Breathing is weak. Blood pressure low, heart rate low. I email my notes to my college friend Stacy, who is now a doctor in Greensboro. She calls my cell: Your dad is super sick. I ask her if he's going to die. She repeats: Your dad is super sick. You need to spend as much time with him right now as you can.

Too sick for this hospital. We must get him back to Durham. Ray leaves to get our mother; I stay with our father.

I am next to him. I am with him. I will not leave him. They put in a central line. They measure him to see if he will fit in the helicopter. He won't fit. He'll have to go in an ambulance. I will go with him. Can I go with him? I won't get in the way. I leave my rental car in the hospital parking lot. He screams when they transfer him to the gurney. Screams as they push him down the hall. Screams as they load him into the ambulance. I watch from the sidewalk, sun warming the top of my head, my face. Perfect weather. Easter Sunday. If he dies on Easter, I can never eat Cadbury Eggs again. I get in the front seat. Moans from the back. Daddy, this is Jennifer. I'm right here. You're not alone. Jennifer is here. You are not alone. The driver gets on I-40 heading east. He wants to talk about ACC basketball. I try to be civil. I can't stop pressing my feet into the floor. Entire body clenched like a fist. This is the new reality. My life in New York is over. My life is here now. In this state. This ambulance. We should be going faster. Why isn't he going faster? Go faster. He misses the exit, has to turn around. My body is shaking, vibrating. No more sound from the back. We pull into the ambulance bay. He screams as they unload him. I follow behind, clutching his CPAP machine to my chest. It's my ticket in. If they try to kick me out I will say, Look—I have his CPAP machine and I know how to hook it up. You need me. We pass through the ER, enter the ICU. Room sixteen. I present the CPAP like an offering. They don't need it. I sit in a chair in the corner behind a big piece of medical equipment. I will keep out of the way. They will let me stay. Most of them don't even notice the daughter in the corner. People come in and out, do things to his body, take blood from his body, look at his body, insert an arterial line. The skin over the bottom of his stomach, near his pelvis, is black. He is mostly unconscious. A short, male surgeon stands in the corner by the door with his arms crossed over his chest, one hand positioned over his mouth, brow furrowed, shaking his head. He doesn't see me. Doesn't know I'm here. Looks perplexed, concerned. I text Ray, who is in the waiting room with our mother: Our lives just changed forever. Brace yourself. My friend Jack in New York texts and asks what he can do: Send angels. We need angels. A doctor finally notices me. He says, Your father is very sick. I say, I know. Will someone please go out and speak with my mother? They can't; too busy. I'm afraid if I leave they won't let me back in. Afraid he'll die alone. But my mother needs to know. I have to be the one to tell her. Before I go, I kiss his forehead, hold his hand, speak into his ear: Daddy, it's Jennifer. I have to go check on Mommy. If you need to let go, you can let go. I really hope you stay, but it's OK if you need to go. I will take care of Mommy and Ray. I'll take care of everyone. Everything. Thank you for being a wonderful father. I love you.

I walk out of the room, out of the ICU, down the hall. I wipe my eyes, my nose. The carpet in the hall is worn thin, ugly, dark blue and gray. I don't know what to say to her. How to tell her. That she's probably about to lose her partner. Her best friend. Forty years together. Forty years. Time slows as I near the waiting room. I hear her voice talking to a stranger. We've been together forty years, she tells him. I want to keep walking, to walk down this hall forever and never reach an end to the walk to my mother to tell her it's over.

I AM NEXT to her. I am with her. I take pictures of her injuries because she tells me to. Bruises on her face. Bruises on her arms. Bruises on her legs. Each bruise a violent rainbow of color: blue, red, yellow, black. Her face is the worst. A thick arch of red extends over her right eyelid and tapers out at an angle just beyond the corner of the eye, like cat eyes drawn on with a wide burgundy brush. She fell on her right side, so the bruising is all on the right. She looks like somebody beat her up, badly. She says, My feet fell out from underneath me, Jennie. I hit my face on the sink in his room. I try to imagine the scene: my mother screaming on the floor, my father in a hospital bed unable to help. Hurts too much to see it, so I stop. Her mind is a pinball, bouncing back and forth across a table: Oh Jennie, what are we going do if he dies? I just don't know what we're going to do. Oh Jennifer, you should see those pussycats—that little gray one is getting to be such a tub. Your father feeds them way too much. Oh honey, your skin looks terrible. Why does your skin look so terrible?

I am still shaking. Jerking. Vibrating, like a bed in a cheap motel. I can't stop. I try lying on the floor of the waiting room and taking slow, deep breaths. Doesn't work; still shaking.

We wait—my mother, my brother, and me. Hours pass. My friend Ginny calls regularly with updates; her father, a doctor at this hospital, calls the ICU to check on my father, then calls Ginny, then Ginny calls me. We are getting more information from a college friend I haven't seen in ten years than from the ICU staff. My friend Kristin is on her way from South Carolina. Afternoon becomes evening, evening becomes night. Nobody left in the waiting room but us.

Kristin calls from outside the hospital: the doors are locked, she can't get in. I meet her and open the door. What do you need me to do? she asks. Keep my mother occupied, I tell her. I can't take care of her right now. Please just keep talking to her. Kristin sits down next to my mother, talks with her about pussycats, death, my terrible skin. Kristin is my hero. A doctor comes out to talk to us. I'm in a tunnel: everything he says reaches me on a delay, echoes off the walls. I hear that my father is very sick. Intubated, sedated, on contact isolation because he could have something called C. diff or MRSA. Heart, lungs, kidneys failing. Septic shock. My mother asks if he is going to be OK. The doctor looks at her like she's dense, slow, stupid. He says my father is so septic that he's foaming at the mouth. His attitude offends me. I don't say anything about it, though, because I can't talk. I'm in a tunnel, far away, shaking. I don't know how to stop shaking. Don't know how I'm going to take care of my mother. Bury my father. Leave New York. Live in North Carolina. Stand up from this chair. The doctor leaves. Crying, confusion, more talk about pussycats. Two surgeons come out close to midnight: Dr. Belfore and another surgeon I've never met. Dr. Belfore is nervous, anxious—not casual and flippant like after the second surgery. She tells us that my father is very sick. She doesn't know what happened, won't know if she can help him until she gets inside him. They will operate tonight. They should know within the first thirty minutes if they can do anything to help him. They tell us we can go back and see him before they take him away, if we'd like.

Ray and I help our mother walk down the hallway with the ugly blue and gray carpet. I pick up the phone by the door, tell them who we are. The doors swing open. Wash your hands in the sink by the door, we are told. We wash our hands in the sink by the door. My mother clings to our arms as we walk to room sixteen. We stand at the threshold of the room. My mother sways and cries. My father lies before us. Tube down his throat. Unconscious. Many lines exit/enter him. They make us put yellow paper gowns over our clothes, blue latex gloves on our hands. I help my mother put on hers. She's shaking, too. We enter the room, surround the bed. His bloated black belly is covered with blankets. The machine breathing for him keeps a steady tempo. He is my father. He is terrycloth robe and slippers shuffling to the front door, locking it before bedtime every night. He is funny daddy, silly daddy tickling me until I pee on the bed. He is daddy-man, calling me down to the den to watch *Doctor Who* and *Star Trek*. He is committed daddy, driving me house to house for trick-or-treat on a rainy Halloween night. He is patient, smart-ass daddy, teaching me parallel parking in an elementary school parking lot. He is Daddy.

Ray is frozen. Mommy pets Daddy's face, arm, hand. Maybe we should pray. Maybe we should say the Lord's Prayer, like we did before bed when we were little. Mommy and I join hands. Ray backs away and stands against the wall, arms folded in front of his chest. Shakes his head no, no, no. Eyes brim with tears. Doesn't want to be touched. His arms seem to hold him together, to prevent him from breaking apart. His lips are pressed together in a thin line. There's violence in his sadness. Mommy and I hold hands and say Our Father, who art in heaven, hallowed be thy name. Thy kingdom come, thy will be done, on earth as it is in heaven. Give us this day our daily bread, and forgive us our debts as we forgive our debtors. And lead us not into temptation, but deliver us from evil. For thine is the kingdom, the power, and the glory, forever and ever. Amen. And then we say goodbye.

# *Valkyrie*

NORTH CAROLINA, DECEMBER 2008

THE THEATER HAS stadium seating, so my parents sit on the ground level in the wheel-chair accessible area because my mother can't climb the stairs. Ray and I sit a few rows behind and above them. My mother has started using a walker, which she positions in front of their two seats. She's using Granny's old walker, which has a flat surface in the middle on which to sit. The previews haven't started yet and the lights are still up in the theater. My father leaves to visit the concession stand. For at least a full five minutes, I watch as people enter the theater, see my mother, and react to her presence. Her body is spilling out of her seat; she is slouched over like an enormous rag doll and her legs are extended straight out into the aisle. She looks sad, forlorn, vulnerable. The expressions on the faces of the people passing by alternate between pity, disgust, and anger. After my father returns and places a large bucket of popcorn on the walker between them, my parents start eating the popcorn and the looks intensify. "How dare they be so fat/take up so much space/eat so much popcorn?" the looks seem to say. They are glares, really. Glares that contain a quiet violence, an instinctual revulsion.

After the lights dim and the previews play, I spend 121 minutes watching Tom Cruise try to kill Hitler. Because I know that the movie is based on a true story, and because I know that Hitler was not assassinated, I surmise from the very outset that Tom Cruise is going to fail and die. But I sit there and watch it anyway.

Later, at my parents' house, I sit on the edge of the bed in the guest room and cry. I haven't seen my parents since last Christmas. They've gained so much weight in the last year. My father looks pregnant; my mother can barely walk. My father hears me crying and comes in the bedroom to investigate. "What's wrong, honey?" he asks. I tell him that we all need to talk. We go to the kitchen. Ray leans on the door frame while my parents and I sit at the table. I tell them that I'm afraid they're going to die—afraid that they're eating themselves to death. I tell them that I'm worried about their diabetes, their sleep apnea, their mobility. My mother gets defensive and accusatory. My father listens and waits for me to finish. I continue to cry. I tell them that I want to do something to help them because I don't want to lose them. My mother says, "Well, if you lived down here and cooked healthy meals for us on a regular basis, then I'm sure we would lose some weight."

My father tells us that he has talked to his doctor about getting gastric bypass surgery and has started the screening process for it. He says he will have to undergo psychiatric evaluations, attend informational classes, and submit to physical exams and tests. If all goes well and he gets approved, he'll have the surgery in Durham, probably sometime next year. I say that I will fly down to help out when he has the surgery. I tell him that I'm proud of him for taking action to improve his health.

# Surgery #3—Darlin', I'm Gonna Give You Two

NORTH CAROLINA, APRIL 2010

DATE OF SURGERY: 04/05/2010

PREOPERATIVE DIAGNOSIS: Sepsis.

POSTOPERATIVE DIAGNOSES:

1. Sepsis secondary to gastrojejunal anastomotic disruption.
2. Jejunal leak on palpation of the jejunal jejunostomy.

DESCRIPTION OF PROCEDURE: The patient was brought to the operating room. General orotracheal anesthesia had already been induced in the intensive care unit. He was transferred to the operative bed and prepped and draped in the usual sterile manner. His previous laparoscopic port sites were accessed and used to place trocars within the abdomen. Upon entry into the abdomen frank abdominal fluid was apparent with a significant rind over most of his bowels. . .

a possible new jejunojejunal leak...

area was oversewn with 2-0 Polysorb suture...

fluid in the abdomen was suctioned and irrigated out of all quadrants and attention was then made to the gastrojejunostomy...

area was very gently identified and with palpation was exposed...

became apparent that there was a large gastrojejunal leak...

looked as if there had been some necrosis at the suture line itself...

this was oversewn to complete a gastrojejunal closure with interrupted Polysorb sutures...

```
considered placing a feeding tube...

felt that a feeding tube [would] have additional risk that was
not warranted in this setting...

patient appeared to tolerate the procedure
```

AFTER EXITING THE ICU, we decide that Ray will stay and the rest of us will go. I haven't slept since Friday night, and Mommy is in pain. Ray will call me when the surgery is over. Kristin drives, Mommy sits in the front seat, I sit in the back. They talk about pussycats. I don't talk. When we get home, Kristin and I crawl into the same bed, like we did during sleepovers when we were young. I can't stop shaking. I ask her to hold me; she does. The shaking doesn't stop. Kristin falls asleep. I don't sleep. My body feels like colors. Fluorescent greens and blues and yellows surge through me in electric beams. They start at my feet, travel up my legs, shoot through my torso, my chest, across my face, and out through my scalp. I am sure that my father is dying and I am feeling it. He is saying goodbye in energy colors. I will go back to the hospital to be with Ray when the surgeons come out and tell him. I get in the shower around 3 a.m. Ray calls at 3:45 as I'm getting ready to leave: Daddy survived the surgery. I drive back to the hospital.

Ray is alone. The waiting room is dark. He tells me that the surgeons found two leaks, fixed them, said they would come out and talk more with us later. I tell Ray to go home and sleep, that I will take over from here. The rest of the day is chaotic, blurry. Ginny's doctor-father finds me in the waiting room after visiting my father and tells me that my father is very sick; Ginny and her husband Ben bring me breakfast. Later, Kristin brings my mother back to the hospital. Stacy (college friend, now doctor in Greensboro) arrives. It is her day off and she has come to help me. (So many people love me. Why do so many people love me?)

Stacy, Mommy, and I go to the ICU to see him. I push Mommy in a wheelchair. We wash our hands in the sink by the door. I help Mommy out of the wheelchair at the threshold of his room. We put on paper gowns and gloves. He looks worse than he did last night. He is surrounded by machines, connected to two IV poles laden with bags and little machines. Mommy trips, screams, almost falls, lands in a chair. A nurse sees my mother's bruises and suggests we take her to the ER. I say no, thank you, she just needs to sit. Stacy stands next to the IV poles and explains what each medication is for. She points at one and says, This one needs to go away. This one is pumping his heart for him. You need to get rid of this one as quickly as possible. We wheel my mother back to the waiting room and wait for Dr. Belfore to come talk to us. Kristin leaves.

Dr. Belfore arrives. She tells us that he had two leaks: one in his small bowel, and one higher up at the juncture where she connected the new stomach pouch to the intestines during the first surgery. She says that almost half the connection had been lost, that it popped open during an eating episode. (But my father hasn't been eating, he's only been drinking liquids. How is this his fault?) She says they will feed him through TPN in lieu of a feeding tube, explains that TPN is administered through his arm. He can have nothing by mouth, not even water. For how long? Don't know. His body is fighting sepsis. He's still intubated, sedated; kidneys aren't making urine. They may start dialysis, but not today.

Dr. Belfore leaves. Stacy leaves. Tim and Thelma, old family friends, arrive. They bring a basket of Easter candy. My mother eats the candy. It is afternoon. I'm still shaking. Tim says, Darlin', come on out to my car so I can give you a Xanax. Tim and I go out to his car. He opens his trunk, pulls out a bag, takes a bottle out of the bag and says, Darlin', I'm gonna give you two. He puts two pills in my hand. Tim and Thelma tell me to go home and sleep, they will sit with my mother. I drive home, take the Xanax, and sleep.

# Losing My Religion

THE FIRST FEW days of my family's disaster felt like one long day. I didn't sleep between Friday night and Monday afternoon when I took the Xanax, so to me it really was one long day. As I sat in the corner of the ICU room during my father's intake that Sunday, I pulled out my journal and wrote the following three lines:

> 4/4/10
> 5:56pm
>
> *My life just changed forever.*
>
> *This is the new reality.*
>
> *Now I know how this feels. Yes.*

The last line was in response to a conversation with a friend that had occurred the week before while I had been back in New York. I told her about the gastric bypass experience—how helpless we all felt when things started going wrong the day after the surgery, how angry and sad I got every time I was around my mother, and how frightened I had been about the possibility of losing my father. She pointed out that now I knew how that felt—how it felt to be so powerless and close to losing my father, intimating that I should view the experience as contributing to my emotional growth, or personal evolution, or something like that.

That Sunday afternoon, when I thought I was watching my father die, I found my friend's guidance to be both ironically prescient and entirely inadequate. Easter weekend of 2010 commenced the most painful, accelerated, and prolonged course in self-growth that I had ever experienced. Practically every day that summer I encountered some experience, emotion, or person that stretched and broke me. And every time I thought that surely things couldn't get worse, surely my family had reached our capacity for misfortune and heartache, a new misfortune or heartache would land on top of the last one, compounding the effects of all that had preceded it. I used to laugh when I'd think about the cliché, "God never gives you more than you can handle" (a phrase that more than a few well-intentioned people said to me that year). My relationship with God/spirituality was in a state of flux that summer, along with everything else. The God that was emerging for me through the cracks and crevices of our everyday disasters seemed darker and crueler than the God that so many people go on and on about.

I suppose the platitude that "God never gives you more than you can handle" was true in a sense: by the end of every day I was decimated, and the next morning I would rebuild myself, growing more expansive and calloused with each daily regeneration, simply because I had no choice. But some days I couldn't handle it. Some days I said and did things that I now regret. Some days I hid. Some nights I drank alone until I passed out. I suppose the veracity of the dictate "God never gives you more than you can handle" depends greatly on your definition of what it means to "handle."

When our disaster started, I had been practicing Nichiren Buddhism for about two years. The practice had initially appealed to me in part because of its emphasis on taking action—by chanting twice a day, setting intentions, and focusing on them, I could change my karma, alter my future, and improve my life, as well as the lives and futures of others. This emphasis on action and the belief that we have the power to alter our fate were instrumental in helping me work up the courage to leave a marriage that wasn't right for me and a job that made me feel trapped and miserable. Two years of chanting "nam-myoho-renge-kyo" twice a day in front of a sacred scroll had helped me get unstuck during a period of great stuckness in my late twenties in New York, so I don't entirely discredit the practice.

Another aspect of Nichiren Buddhism that I found beneficial was the guidance to chant for the happiness of your enemies—the people who piss you off, hurt you, make your life difficult. If you want to improve a troubled relationship, I was told, then you must chant for that person's happiness. I chanted every day, twice a day, for my mother's happiness. I chanted until I cried. Until I was hoarse. I chanted for the ability to love her and have empathy for her, no matter what she did or said. I chanted for the ability to communicate with her in a space beyond the years of anger and resentment between us—to return to a time when the only emotion that passed between us was love. I chanted so fucking much for that. And when I was far away from her, it really helped. I was able to tap into the bottomless bucket of love for her that I discovered I possessed once I was an adult. I could empathize with her so much that it would bring me to tears. Yet every time I saw her or spoke to her on the phone, we fell right back into the deep grooves of our dysfunctional relationship.

But that wasn't the reason why I stopped practicing Nichiren Buddhism. I stopped because once my father's battle for life commenced, I felt uncomfortable every time I sat down at my altar to chant. I knew that I was supposed to chant for him to live, to heal, to overcome. But every time I did, it felt wrong—borderline dangerous. Perhaps he wasn't supposed to survive, I thought, and by chanting for him to live I could be fucking with some sort of cosmic, karmic course that just needed to play out. Who was I to play God, to effect change in the universe when I could only see what was in front of me and my own selfish desires? I finally decided that if he was supposed to die, he was supposed to die. I would do everything in my power to prevent that from happening, but I wouldn't try to mess with his (or my) cosmic path anymore.

I suppose that the biggest spiritual takeaway for me from that summer was the confirmation that we are not in control. I'm not sure who (or what) is, but it sure as hell isn't me. And it certainly isn't my father. It isn't even Dr. Belfore, a highly trained, experienced surgeon and renowned expert in her field. We are all either floating in the aether of chaos, or acting out some grand master narrative compelled by invisible forces. Based on the way my 2010 played out, my money's on a combination of the two.

# He Which Hath No Stomach to This Fight

NORTH CAROLINA, APRIL 2010

```
CONSULTATION REPORT: 04/07/2010

We are asked by Dr. ————— to see Mr. Blevins to help in
the management of his renal insufficiency and associate issues.
He is an unfortunate 61-year-old gentleman who had a Roux-en-Y
weight loss reduction surgery on March 24th and presented now,
first to ————— County and now to here in septic shock...

Acute renal failure, ATN secondary to sepsis is likely...

The patient remains critically ill. The case discussed at length
with daughter and she would want dialysis and other aggressive
measures done if appropriate. I also discussed the risks and
benefits of central line placement to do dialysis.
```

A PHONE CALL wakes me up from my Xanax-induced nap around dinnertime. It's Jack, my best friend in New York. He tells me that he just bought a plane ticket, that he'll be here tomorrow. He says he's coming to take care of me while I take care of everyone else. I sit on the floor of my parents' guest room and sob. Jack is coming. My friend is coming. (Why do so many people love me?)

The next day, Ray and I drive to the airport. He drives his car; I drive my rental car, which has been sitting in the hospital parking lot in Burlington since Sunday morning. My cell phone rings as I'm walking out of the rental car place. It's someone from my new job in New York. They ask me a question, but I can't hear it because of a plane flying overhead. I ask them to repeat the question. They ask me about a FedEx package I sent last week—they want to know where the receipt is. I had forgotten that the world was still turning, that other people's lives have been proceeding normally, sensibly. I'm annoyed. As another plane passes over my head, I tell them that I don't know, that my father is probably dying, and that I can't help them right now. Ray and I drive to the terminal, park, go inside and wait for Jack. I see him (tall, bespectacled, wearing a backpack) from afar, walking through the TSA point-of-no-return checkpoint. We meet in the middle of the terminal, and I fall into his hug. He says, "Hey, buddy. How you doing?" I say, "Friend, I am so fucking glad you're here."

We head to the hospital. Jack asks when's the last time I ate. I tell him I don't know. We drive through a Chick-fil-A. I eat half of my sandwich. When we get to the hospital, Tim and Thelma are in the waiting room. Thelma tells us that the kidney doctor, who I met yesterday, had come out to speak with the family earlier and spoke with them instead. Thelma asked him, in his opinion, what are Jim's odds of survival. He didn't want to say. She assured him that he could be honest because they weren't family, just close friends. He told them that yesterday he would have said the odds were forty-sixty, but today the odds are more like fifty-fifty. They're prepping him for dialysis but aren't going to start it yet.

I head back to the ICU to see him, alone. I arm myself with a small bundle of papers folded and tucked into the back pocket of my jeans. Once they let me in, I wash my hands in the sink by the door, walk down the hall to room sixteen, put on a gown and gloves, and enter. I stand by the head of the bed, take the papers from my back pocket, lean into his ear, and read "Invictus":

Out of the night that covers me,
    Black as the pit from pole to pole,
I thank whatever gods may be
    For my unconquerable soul.

In the fell clutch of circumstance
    I have not winced nor cried aloud.
Under the bludgeonings of chance
    My head is bloody, but unbowed.

Beyond this place of wrath and tears
    Looms but the Horror of the shade,
And yet the menace of the years
    Finds and shall find me unafraid.

It matters not how strait the gate,
    How charged with punishments the scroll,
I am the master of my fate,
    I am the captain of my soul.

Various machines throughout the ICU beep and chirp, as if they're communicating. As if they're issuing mating calls. The room is dark and overly warm. Out in the hall, a respiratory technician pushes a cart past the door. I read "Jabberwocky":

'Twas brillig, and the slithy toves
    Did gyre and gimble in the wabe:
All mimsy were the borogoves,
    And the mome raths outgrabe.

"Beware the Jabberwock, my son!
    The jaws that bite, the claws that catch!
Beware the Jubjub bird, and shun
    The frumious Bandersnatch!"

He took his vorpal sword in hand;
    Long time the manxome foe he sought—
So rested he by the Tumtum tree
    And stood awhile in thought.

And, as in uffish thought he stood,
    The Jabberwock, with eyes of flame,
Came whiffling through the tulgey wood,
    And burbled as it came!

One, two! One, two! And through and through
    The vorpal blade went snicker-snack!
He left it dead, and with its head
    He went galumphing back.

"And hast thou slain the Jabberwock?
    Come to my arms, my beamish boy!
O frabjous day! Callooh! Callay!"
    He chortled in his joy.

Heat emanates from his body. He has a fever of 104. They've put ice blankets on top and underneath him to try to cool him down, but it doesn't seem to be working. Being near him causes my temperature to rise. I start to sweat. The fever means that his body is fighting the sepsis.

I want to inspire him to keep fighting. I read one of his favorites, from *Henry V*:

If we are mark'd to die, we are enow
To do our country loss; and if to live,
The fewer men, the greater share of honour.
God's will! I pray thee, wish not one man more.
By Jove, I am not covetous for gold,
Nor care I who doth feed upon my cost;
It yearns me not if men my garments wear;
Such outward things dwell not in my desires:
But if it be a sin to covet honour,
I am the most offending soul alive.
No, faith, my coz, wish not a man from England:
God's peace! I would not lose so great an honour
As one man more, methinks, would share from me
For the best hope I have. O, do not wish one more!
Rather proclaim it, Westmoreland, through my host,
That he which hath no stomach to this fight,
Let him depart; his passport shall be made
And crowns for convoy put into his purse:
We would not die in that man's company
That fears his fellowship to die with us.
This day is called the feast of Crispian:
He that outlives this day, and comes safe home,
Will stand a tip-toe when the day is named,
And rouse him at the name of Crispian.
He that shall live this day, and see old age,
Will yearly on the vigil feast his neighbours,
And say "To-morrow is Saint Crispian:"
Then will he strip his sleeve and show his scars.
And say "These wounds I had on Crispin's day."

Tubes coming out of his abdomen drain bloody fluid into little plastic bulbs the size of goose eggs laying on the bed beside him. His wrists are strapped to the bed, a precaution in case he suddenly becomes conscious and tries to pull the intubation tube out of his throat. But he's sedated, so he won't. His eyes are slightly open. He is here and not here. He is on the battlefield between life and death.

I believe that he can hear me because I have to. If he knows he's not alone, if he knows that he is loved, then he will fight. I know this because I know him. I know that he's afraid of failure, afraid of disappointing us. And I know that he covets distinction. He is King Henry, heading into battle as the underdog. Jim Blevins would wish not one man more. He will want to one day strip his sleeve and show his scars. He and I are alike in this regard. We both love a challenge.

The next day is Wednesday. Ray takes our mother to a doctor to further assess the injuries she sustained when she fell in the hospital in Burlington on Saturday. He calls me with the report: the doctor determined that she broke the orbital bone above one of her eyes and needs surgery, or else her face will start to cave in. After hanging up the phone, I lie down on the floor of the ICU waiting room and start laughing. Jack looks up from his laptop and asks what's up. "Bring it on," I say. "All of it. I want locusts. I want frogs. I want an ancient demon to spring forth from the bowels of the earth in front of the hospital so I can battle it like Gandalf. You shall not pass, mother fucker."

Later, in the car on our way to dinner, the emergency broadcasting system starts bleating over the radio: a tornado warning. Bring it.

# Brother from Another Mother

JACK STAYED WITH us for almost a week. Like Kristin (who's been in my life since the eighth grade), he's always felt more like a sibling than a friend. I met him in August of 2000, shortly after I graduated college, when we were interns at a professional regional theater. We'd known each other for less than a month when we decided to adopt a cat together, whom we named El Gato del Fuego. We were both only making $150 a week and couldn't afford the adoption fee at the time, so I put the cost of Gato's adoption on my credit card and Jack paid me his half later. We lived across the hall from each other in actor housing and split our time with Gato, who would let us know every few days when she was ready to switch parents by sitting at the door of whichever room she was in and meowing. Jack and I would open our doors, and Gato would walk across the hall to her other person. We struck a deal that the one who stayed at the theater longer would keep Gato. I left first, so Gato became Jack's.

Jack is a golden human being. He's just…golden. Despite (or, perhaps because of) the many hardships he's endured since he was a kid, he has a brilliant and acerbic wit that can create moments of hilarity in the darkest hours. And he's shown up for my darkest hours—sitting with me all night in the ER waiting room of a Brooklyn hospital after I got hit by a car, rushing to my aid and helping me move the day I left my ex-husband and my movers fell through, hopping on a flight down to North Carolina the week my whole world fell apart. And on all of my darkest, most horrible days, he has managed to make me laugh.

One night during the week that he stayed with us, Jack made dinner for my mother, Ray, and me. As Jack was dishing the stir-fry onto plates, Ray and I attempted to clear off some space on the kitchen table where we could eat. My parents were kind of living like hoarders at the time. The kitchen table was piled high with all kinds of crap— bills and assorted papers, small baskets full of medications, random pieces of medical equipment, and other curious items of miscellanea, like a Furby. We stacked most of the stuff on the floor, pushing the rest into the center of the table. "Bring me a bottle of water," my mother commanded from her seat at the table, and Jack gave me a look as he reached into the fridge to get the water. As soon as my mother saw her plate, she started picking out all of the pieces of bell pepper and said, "Oh, I can't eat peppers.

They'll kill me. They're really very, very bad for me." After a long, emotional day around my mother, my patience was depleted. I sighed and stared at the pill bottles and box of Band-Aids sitting in the middle of the table, longing to run away from the mess of my life. There was a long, tense pause, then Jack said, "Hey Blevvy, will you please pass the Band-Aids?" I instinctively reached for the box, and then stopped when I realized he was joking. We all burst out laughing—even my mother.

Until that week, Jack had only ever met my mother in passing. After spending about five or six days with us, he assessed my relationship with my mother quite astutely. He said, "Blev, she treats you like you're a sibling she's jealous of or threatened by—not like a daughter she loves."

It was probably the most spot-on observation anyone had ever made regarding our relationship, and I felt like it also applied to the relationship between my mother and Granny. The mother/daughter trilogy in our house seemed to be fueled by both ire and love, perhaps in equal measure. There was an odd sense of being complicit in each other's fates—as if the ship was going down (perpetually going down), and in order to be good daughters and/or mothers we not only had to go down with it, we had to refrain from doing anything to prevent its sinking. My father's medical disaster of 2010 revealed this dynamic perhaps more so than anything that preceded it. And this time my father wasn't around to intervene.

# Legacy

NOWHERE AND EVERYWHERE, 1910–2014

MOMMY RESIDES IN a world beyond blame. She sits atop a mountain of misery, looking down on all of the people who have wronged her, angry that none of them bring her food. So she is forced to eat fast food three meals a day, primarily because her daughter is a selfish, ungrateful bitch who doesn't care about her mother. The evidence of my neglect collects in the floorboards of the car: McDonald's bags full of empty wrappers, a footlong box from Cook Out that once housed a hot dog, Bojangles biscuit boxes licked clean of all remains. Her knees hurt and her back hurts and her neck hurts and surely she has a sinus infection and a heart infection and a brain infection and a yeast infection and why doesn't anyone help her? Why doesn't her daughter help her?! All she ate today was Jell-O and that's her daughter's fault.

Granny's mountain sits next to Mommy's mountain and I climb up there to tend to her feet. I kneel on the floor in front of Granny's chair and put bandages and socks and shoes on her crusty, deformed feet. She talks down to me from her chair, listing all of the things that are my mother's fault and worrying about fat. "Jenn-i-fuh, your parents are gettin' so FAT. What are we gonna do?" And then after Granny dies in 2003, my parents get even fatter.

And then eleven years later, Mommy dies and the man from the crematorium tells us that he has to charge us an extra $300 because she weighs more than 300 pounds. And we have no choice but to pay the money. And when I say goodbye to her body, I put one hand on her stomach and the other on my heart, and I forgive us both.

# No Exit

NORTH CAROLINA, MARCH 2010

WHILE WE WAITED together during my father's first surgery, my mother ate. She filled her purse with snacks from the vending machines while I was in the bathroom. She shoved the food into her mouth with a maniacal intensity. Cashews cascaded down the front of her shirt. She wrapped a Snickers bar in a tissue and attempted to eat it without me noticing, even though I was sitting right next to her. When I said something (I don't remember what—probably something snarky like "You're *still* eating?" or "I can smell the chocolate from here, you know"), she responded with a "Go easy on me today, Jennifer. Alright?! Take it easy on me." Or maybe it was a "I'm doing the *best* I can, Jennifer. Alright?! Just leave me the hell alone." Both were familiar refrains from my childhood and adolescence.

In that moment, as I witnessed my mother's binge, I felt like I was watching one parent chain smoke while the other one was having a cancerous lung removed. But time, distance, and death have revised those feelings and widened my perspective. My mother's need (*need*) to eat with such rapacity and zeal is akin to my need (yes, *need*) to wake up early every morning (usually around 4:30 or 5:00 a.m.) to go to the gym. Interestingly, ironically, my need may be the unintended offspring of hers.

For well over a decade now, my early morning workouts have served many functions. They are both how I take care of myself and how I punish myself. They are simultaneously a joy and a crutch. If I must abstain for a day, I grow anxious, agitated, and pissy. If I must abstain for more than a day, I feel unmoored, desperate, and angry. A practice that began as a way of losing weight eventually evolved into a way of caring for myself, but now borders on addiction.

I work out when I'm injured, sick, hungover. When I've only had a few hours of sleep, or even less than that. My workouts are my way of not becoming my mother, yet, in a sense, they are me becoming my mother.

My mother used food to take care of herself and to punish herself. Food was both a joy and a crutch. And since she grew up listening to Granny tell her that she was too fat and needed to eat less, perhaps her food consumption was *her* way of not becoming her mother.

While she sat next to me eating her tissue-encased Snickers bar, I mentally planned my workouts for the following week, when I would be back in New York: barre class on Monday and Friday, cycling on Tuesday and Thursday, Pilates on Wednesday, kickboxing and weight training on Saturday, and yoga on Sunday. On a day when we both felt distinctly powerless, we sat a few inches apart from each other on a waiting room couch and retreated to the obsessions that comforted us and gave us a sense of control. Just because my addiction is considered "healthy" and appropriate by current cultural standards doesn't make it any less of a crutch than my mother's compulsive eating.

Of course, it didn't occur to either of us to talk about the feelings of powerlessness and anxiety we were both experiencing while someone we loved was undergoing surgery. Our relationship had never been a safe space in which to discuss our feelings; it was more like a minefield we both tried to avoid. So she ate while I daydreamed about future workouts—both of us becoming our mothers as we tried to avoid becoming our mothers.

# The Crossing

NEW YORK, 2005

AFTER I HAD lived in New York for about a year, my father visited me. Prior to his visit, he requested that we go to the Natural History Museum together while he was there. I was worried about him being able to handle the physical demands of the subway system, so we took a cab instead.

As we walked through the exhibits, he sweated profusely and wheezed like an asthmatic. Once the strongest person in my world, my father couldn't even make it through the dinosaur room without having to rest on a bench. At one point during our museum visit, I stepped out into the hall so he wouldn't see me cry. That evening at dinner, I asked the question I had always been too afraid to ask: "What are we going to do about taking care of Mommy if something happens to you?" Without hesitation, he replied: "We will cross that bridge when we get to it." He indicated that the discussion was over by pouring himself another glass of sangria and changing the subject.

Five years later as I stood on the sidewalk in front of the Burlington hospital on Easter Sunday and watched paramedics load my screaming father into an ambulance, I realized that he had used the wrong pronoun that night. What he really meant was "*You* will cross that bridge when *you* get to it," because the crossing, by its very nature, must happen without him.

# Gut

NORTH CAROLINA AND NEW YORK, APRIL 2010

MY FATHER'S TEMPERATURE hovered between 102 and 104 degrees for days. His life-long best friend Russell flew out from California two days after the emergency surgery to see him. I hadn't seen Russell since I was a small child, so it took me a minute to locate him in the waiting room. I brought him back to the ICU and oriented him to the protocol (i.e., wash hands in the sink by the door, put on a gown and gloves before entering the room). When we walked into the room, Russell sidled up next to the bed and said, "Hey, Monk. It's me." "Monk" was my father's nickname in high school, apparently due to his ability to scamper about on the floor in a squatting position, walking on his knuckles and imitating a monkey.

As the two of us sat side by side next to the bed and talked, Russell and I could feel the heat radiating from my father's body. His white blood cell count had come down considerably, but his body was still fighting infection. He was on an array of antibiotics and antifungals. Doctors said that he had yeast in his blood (candidemia). They had inserted a PICC line in his upper arm through which to administer TPN (total parenteral nutrition), but they did not want to give him any nutrition until they got to the root of the infection. He went weeks without receiving any form of nutrition. A consultation report written by an infectious disease specialist dated April 13, 2010 notes that my father was "malnourished." The extended period of malnourishment would have consequences later on.

The same consultation report reads, "he has 3 different gut organisms growing. Based on all these issues it again seems most likely to me that the source of his infection is his gut." Of course, as the report also notes, "he does have known and proven gut leakage."

Later that week as my father's leaky gut continued to fight infection, my gut was telling me that I needed to figure out my immediate future. I had left New York so abruptly. My employer had been supportive and understanding (especially given the fact that I had only worked there for about a month and a half before suddenly disappearing), but I knew that it was just a matter of time before I would lose that job if I didn't go back and at least show my face in the office. Also, I had only packed a few changes of clothes. Jack kept reminding me gently (as I had asked him to) that I had a life elsewhere. So it was decided that Ray would take a few more days off of work and I would go back to New York to pack more clothes and meet with my boss. When I said goodbye to my father, he was still intubated and sedated.

Jack and I boarded a plane back to New York on April 11, exactly one week after my early morning Easter flight. Our friend Moni picked us up at LaGuardia and drove us home. Moni didn't ask any questions, didn't make me talk about the situation I had just left in North Carolina. We rode together in silence. I have always been grateful to her for that silence.

My apartment was a mess. I had packed and left so quickly. A drying rack full of clean clothes was still sitting in the middle of the floor. The morning after my return to New York, I tried to be normal. I got up early and went to a barre class, after not working out for a week. For the first time ever, I had to leave the class early because I couldn't get through it. I sat on a bench in the locker room, afraid I was going to pass out. When I had stepped on the scale before leaving my apartment that morning, I discovered that I had lost about six pounds in the past week. It was stupid of me to try to jump back into my usual workout routine, but I couldn't help it. I wanted so desperately to pretend, for just an hour, that everything was fine and that my life could proceed normally. I managed to shower and get dressed, even though I felt like I was moving in slow motion. When the receptionist saw me walk through the front door of the office, she said, "Oh my God. You look like a ghost. Are you OK?"

I was home by lunchtime. My boss told me that I didn't need to be there—that I should go home and take care of myself. He told me that they could hold my job for a short period (without pay) while I tended to my family crisis in North Carolina. After six years of struggling in New York City, I had finally landed a job with a decent salary that I actually kind of wanted to do. And, for the first time ever, I even had my own office (with a window). I wanted to find a way to hold on to that job.

One day later, my father was extubated. I flew back to North Carolina the following day. I bought a one-way ticket and packed enough clothes for a month. On the day I flew back, Ray took our mother to the surgery to repair her broken orbital bone. Shortly thereafter, I told Ray that he should go back to his job. "One of us should remain employed," I said.

# I Would Like to Speak with a Cup of Tea

## NORTH CAROLINA, APRIL 2010

04/16/2010: Did well overnight, mild confusion . . . wants to get out of bed

04/17/2010: Confused overnight . . . confusion persists

04/18/2010: still somewhat delerious [sic]

04/22/2010: AMS [altered mental status] continues, although pt does now state his daughters [sic] name which is an improvement.

WHEN I RETURN, he is very glad to see me. He is Daddy, but he is not quite Daddy. He sounds like Daddy. He still talks like an attorney—measured, logical, intelligent—but sometimes the things he says are nonsensical. He seems incapable of comprehending what has happened to him. On my first day back, he tells Ray and me, "I will agree to stay here one more night under the following conditions," and then lists his conditions. He wants to get out of bed, but the nurses and doctors won't let him. We keep trying to explain to him that he can't go home tomorrow—that he probably won't be going home for quite some time, but he doesn't get it. He dictates a list of things he wants brought from home. He tells us to reorganize and tidy up the room. He directs us as we do it.

But more than anything, he asks for something to drink. He begs us for it. He tries to trick us into giving it to him. He says, "I would like to speak with a cup of tea." Ray and I try not to laugh. I ask him if that's what he really meant, and he looks at me as if I'm an idiot and repeats (with gusto), "I would like to speak with a cup of tea." I explain to him again why he can't have any. "You have a leak in your new stomach pouch," I tell him. "You almost died. If you consume anything by mouth, you might almost die again." "When can I eat and drink again?" he asks. He asks and asks and asks. "I don't know," I tell him. "I'm so sorry, Daddy, but I don't know." I keep rewetting the little green swab on a stick that he's permitted to suck. He sucks it with gusto.

"Where's Mommy?" he keeps asking. We keep explaining: "She fell in your hospital room in Burlington the day before Easter and broke her orbital bone. She had surgery to fix it. She's at home recovering." He is able to retain the information for a few minutes at a time. He feels bad about her fall, like it was his fault. He's worried about her. Five minutes later, he has forgotten the information again. "Where's your mother?"

Ray returns to his job and life in the mountains of North Carolina, about three and a half hours away. I take over all parental care. He asks if I'm sure about this, and I say yes, we have no choice. I don't want him to lose his job. Someone needs to manage the situation, and our mother is not emotionally or physically capable of doing it. I will fall on the grenade. I believe that my father would do the same.

In the days that follow, we fall into a strange sense of normalcy. I spend my days by his side in a green vinyl recliner. We watch TV. We have conversations that grow crazier every day. I rewet the swab. I rub his feet. He asks me to pick his nose for him; I do it. He asks me to readjust his scrotum; I call a nurse.

# I Do Not Fear Death Itself

I REMEMBER STRUGGLING to explain to people who didn't know my father that the man in the hospital bed was not my father. My father is smart, reasonable, witty, and well-spoken. He has multiple graduate degrees. He possesses a deadpan sarcasm that can be both endearing and enraging. He doesn't lose his temper. As he started losing his mind, some of the doctors, nurses, and nurses' aides who hadn't known him before he lost his mind seemed to just dismiss him as simpleminded. Not that bright. To some degree, they infantilized him long before the "altered mental status" kicked in, with their baby voices and patronizing comments. After the first surgery at the end of March, one day my father remarked, "The pain makes me hurt—it doesn't make me stupid" as a particularly condescending nurse walked out of his room.

I tried to be his flag-bearer. During periods when he was crazy or unconscious, I told the people taking care of him who he was and what he did before he became a lunatic or vegetable in a bed. I wanted them to be invested in his care—to know whose life they were saving. Later when he became violent and combative, I would tell them that I had only seen him lose his temper maybe twice while I was growing up. No, he's never thrown an electric toothbrush at my head before, I would say. Never told me I was a disappointment who was ruining his life. Never thought I was in cahoots with the devil to blow up a hospital. Nope, this is all new, I would say. And this is not Jim Blevins.

Which was tragic, because Jim Blevins was the one person in the world I really needed to talk to. I had so many questions for him. I needed his help, his advice. Also, I needed him to tell me where the fuck he had put all of our family's legal documents. In the week following the near-fatal Easter Sunday, I searched all over my parents' house for my father's power of attorney, living will, and will. My mother thought they were somewhere in the office, so Jack and I tore that office apart. We couldn't find anything. I mean, he's *a freaking attorney*, I thought. Surely those documents are *somewhere*.

I finally managed to log in to his computer. I got really excited when I found a folder named "Important Family Documents." When I opened the folder, I discovered that it only contained one document: the recipe for Granny's turkey stuffing. Of course. Of course our important family document would be a recipe for stuffing. Of course.

We did finally find the documents (I can't remember where or when). In a living will dated December 18, 1989, my father states:

> I, James Ray Blevins, being of sound mind, desire that my life not be prolonged by extraordinary means if my condition is determined to be terminal and incurable. I am aware and understand that this writing authorizes a physician to withhold or discontinue extraordinary means.
>
> It is my belief that death is as much a reality as birth, growth, maturity and old age – it is the one certainty of life. If the time comes when I can no longer take part in decisions for my own future, let this declaration stand as my desire for a natural death. I do not fear death itself as much as I fear the indignities of deterioration, dependence and hopeless pain.
>
> This declaration is made after careful consideration. I recognize that this appears to place a heavy responsibility upon those who care for me, but it is with the intention of relieving them of such responsibility and of placing it upon myself in accordance with my strong convictions that this declaration is made.

He fears "the indignities of deterioration, dependence, and hopeless pain." I thought a lot about this document in June when we reached the point where we had to make a very difficult decision. When the one person I wanted to consult about the decision, the man I sat next to eight hours a day, didn't even know who I was.

# Parent

NORTH CAROLINA, APRIL 2010

HE DOESN'T KNOW who I am, doesn't know where he is. Slack-jawed, eyelids drooping, he begs for food and water that I can't give him. But today he's not begging. He's not even talking. His head occasionally rolls and falls, like he's a newborn baby with jelly muscles.

I'm worried that he's had a stroke. My intelligent, articulate father now raves like a lunatic and looks through me as if I were a stranger, or a ghost. When I spoke to one of the surgeons on the phone yesterday about the possibility of a stroke, she told me that it might help to bring in photo albums. "Showing him old family pictures may help stimulate his cognitive functions," she said.

I sit in the green vinyl recliner next to his bed and flip through my childhood. When I find a photo I think he'll like, I take it out of the protective plastic, hold it up in front of his lolling head, and tell him what he's seeing. "Look, Daddy: our old house in Breckenridge." "Look, Daddy: Easter egg hunt in Danbrooke Park."

I come across images I didn't even know existed. In one, we're at a small fair or festival in the parking lot of a strip mall in Winston-Salem. It looks like I'm about four years old and Ray is about three. The three of us are sitting together in a tiny car in some sort of children's ride—it looks like part of a little train that takes kids around the parking lot. I marvel at how skinny my father is in the picture, at his ability to fit in that little car. He doesn't seem to have an ounce of fat on his body.

I show him the picture, but it elicits no response. None of them do. He rolls his head in my direction and rests his glassy, watery eyes on my face. I feel old and alone. Somehow the four-year-old in the picture is now thirty-one and able to drive and divorce and watch people die. I feel like there's no ground anymore. I walk on something other than ground. I don't float, because I'm too heavy to float—too burdened, too anxious. I am weighted down to ground that isn't there. It's the sensation of sitting in the front car of a roller coaster and pressing my feet down as hard as I can into the bottom of the car as we crest the top of the hill and begin the steep descent down. Since Easter I've been pressing my feet into false ground, and my stomach has been living in my throat.

I spend my days with my father and my nights with my mother. When I leave the hospital at the end of each day, I stop at Whole Foods or another grocery store to buy something healthy that my mother and I can eat for dinner. I've also started buying a single piece of cake for us to split for dessert. Then I make the thirty-five-minute drive from Durham to Burlington in rush hour traffic. When I enter the house, my mother is always in her pink recliner, covered in blankets and cats, watching television or sleeping. She's still recovering from the surgery. Since her surgery, she has only been to the hospital a few times to see my father. Most days I beg her to stay home so I only have to take care of one parent at a time. The unfortunate side effect of this has been increased delusional thinking. She believes he's going to come home any day now, and every night I must re-explain the severity of the situation.

As I empty the contents of the grocery bag onto the kitchen table, she pushes the switch on the recliner's handheld control, which slowly lowers the legs of the chair as it raises her body up to an almost standing position. My father has a matching blue recliner that sits next to her pink one; they bought them at a medical supply store a few years ago when it started getting too difficult for them to get in and out of chairs. As she uses the walker to make her way over to the table, she talks in a non-sequitur flurry. "Oh, you should have seen those pussycats today...they both slept on me all day! Oh Jennifer, I don't know what we're going to do if your father dies! I just don't know what we'll do! Did you get us something good to eat, or did you get us another one of those salads with weeds in it?"

I update her on his condition as we eat. She feels bad for not coming with me today, and I try to explain that he wouldn't have even known who she was if she had. She doesn't understand, doesn't seem to believe me. She doesn't seem capable of seeing him the way that I saw him today. When we finish dinner, I pull the piece of strawberry layer cake out of the bag and place it between us. "Ooo! They had that cake again today, huh?! It's sinful how delicious it is!" she says. We both dig our forks in and get a bite. With her mouth full of cake, she says, "You'd better stop buying this cake. You're gonna get fat."

# Medical Records Medley

NORTH CAROLINA, APRIL 2010

```
EXAMINATION: 8183 - PELVIC WITHOUT CONTRAST CT    Apr 19 2010
REASON: JEJUNAL LEAK
GASTRIC LEAK
```

...findings are suspicious for persistent contrast leak.

HE'S STILL LEAKING. The surgeons hope that the leak will heal on its own without further surgery. Dr. Belfore tells me that they could insert a stent, a small piece of tubing that looks like Chinese finger cuffs, which would let fluid pass through without leaking out, allowing the tissue surrounding the leak to heal. But she tells me that they're not going to do it yet. Another surgery is not a viable option right now because his tissue is fragile and they're afraid his body couldn't withstand another surgery. "So what can we do?" I ask. We can wait, I am told.

I ask the doctors what's wrong with my father's mind. They don't know. Maybe it's his electrolytes, they tell me. Potassium levels. Something like that. "Could it be a stroke?" I ask. It's possible, they tell me.

```
EXAMINATION: 8027 - HEAD W/O CONTRAST CT    Apr 23 2010
REASON: CONFUSION
HISTORY: Transient alteration of awareness.
```

...No acute intracranial abnormality.

It's not a stroke. Some of the ICU doctors and nurses say that it could be ICU delirium. Apparently being stuck in an ICU room twenty-four hours a day often causes patients to go temporarily insane. One of the fellows on Dr. Belfore's team tells me that sometimes the body gets so sick that the sickness affects the mind, and that once they solve the problem in the body, the mind will go back to normal. But everyone just seems to be guessing. No one can tell me for sure when or if I will ever get my father back. My anger increases daily.

EXAMINATION: 8183 - PELVIC WITHOUT CONTRAST CT     Apr 23 2010
REASON: POSSIBLE BLEEDING

...suspicious for blood within the excluded portion of the
stomach.


They think he's bleeding in his remnant stomach—the ninety percent of his stomach that was left over after creating his new stomach pouch during the gastric bypass procedure. He may have developed a bleeding ulcer in the "excluded" stomach, they tell me.

*Excluded* (verb, past tense): omitted, prohibited, precluded, ostracized, barred, banned, rejected. This stomach is not welcome; it has been excluded. And now it is festering, rebelling, haunting. The return of the repressed?


EXAMINATION: 7103 - CXR PORTABLE EXAM     Apr 25 2010
REASON: R/O PULM EDEMA

...The PICC line is poorly visualized secondary to the patient's
very large body habitus and the portable technique...


Yes, my father is fat. His body habitus is large. But "very large"? Really? Then what would you call a 500-pound body? A 600-pound body? An 800-pound body? They exist, you know. And they need adequate medical care. And how those bodies became that large doesn't matter. It's irrelevant. Regardless of the history of the fat, I can promise you that the stories of those bodies are more complicated than you have the ability to comprehend. You, radiologist, reader of pictures. You who sees bodies as black-and-white and two-dimensional. You who evaluates the insides of strangers. You who have probably never been "very large." My father's body is not an obstacle, and his fat does not exist to spite you. If you are unable to visualize my father's PICC line, if you are unable to perform your job because of the size of his "body habitus" and the "portable technique," then perhaps you should develop a new technique. And get better at your fucking job.

```
EXAMINATION: 7103 - CXR PORTABLE EXAM      Apr 26 2010
REASON: RESPIRATORY DISTRESS
```

Study is limited by body habitus. Depth of inspiration is shallow...Increasing bilateral airspace disease consistent with pneumonia or atelectasis.

You see, here's the thing: We are all limited by body habitus. The fragile, leaky, mushy, mortal body is the one limitation we all share. Those tired, labored lungs in my father's chest that are collapsing and inflamed and filling with fluid, those are your lungs, too. The act of breathing, currently compromised by those failing lungs, is necessary for your survival, too. The pierceable skin, the delicate tissue, the breakable bones, the fickle organs, the susceptible brain—all limiting, all aspects of being alive.

You say that your study of my father's body is limited by my father's body. No, *my father* is limited by his body, as you are by yours. Your study is limited because the medical industry has long privileged certain body types when designing tests, procedures, equipment, and education. This limitation exemplifies a history of fat discrimination that follows us even here—to a hospital that specializes in weight loss surgery for the morbidly obese. Your study is limited because the way that the medical community perceives fat bodies has been limited. My father's body is simply my father's body—finite, precarious, and loved.

# Not Quite Human

BEFORE MY FATHER'S gastric bypass experience, I hated fat in the same way that every red-blooded American citizen is supposed to hate fat. I believed what I was told about fat by the medical community, pop culture, and my mother and Granny—that fat is both unsightly and unhealthy, and that I should stop at nothing in my effort to banish it from my body.

In addition to keeping a journal since I was a child, I have always been a diligent and insatiable student. So when fat started figuring so prominently in my life, I decided to research it. Not just the mainstream, party line about "obesity"—I wanted to dig deeper and find out where our deeply rooted, cultural fear of fat came from. I suspected that the story of American fat was more complex than it appeared, and I discovered that I was right.

Historical documents, which range from magazine advertisements and articles to cartoons to medical literature, reveal that fat stigma in the United States did not emerge as a result of concerns over potential health risks. Prior to the Industrial Revolution, a fat body was a sign of affluence and privilege. But by the late 1800s, the fat body had become a sign of an individual's inability to moderate their enjoyment of the pleasures of modernity. In *Fat Shame: Stigma and the Fat Body in American Culture*, Amy Erdman Farrell argues that our society's obsession with body size and fatness has "inherent connections to fundamental beliefs about race, class, and the evolutionary 'fitness' for citizenship." In other words, woven into the fabric of the collective American unconscious is the belief that fat people are not fit to be citizens and therefore don't deserve the same opportunities and protections granted to "normal" sized and thin Americans. Consequently, "fat people are often treated as *not quite human*, entities to whom the normal standards of polite and respectful behavior do not seem to apply."

Fat hatred has practically become a core American value. As the country grew into an industrialized superpower, the vilification of fat grew right along with it. As unprecedented numbers of Jewish, Irish, and Eastern and Southern European immigrants came to the US in the late nineteenth and early twentieth centuries, they were greeted with prejudice and scorn. Fat ethnic jokes became commonplace, and cartoonists from this era often depicted immigrants as obese and lazy. A "true," native-born American was thin, civilized, and intelligent, whereas an immigrant was fat, primitive, and stupid. (In the early twenty-first century, fat still gets racially coded. Since the "obesity epidemic" is frequently associated with persons of color and the poor, some argue that the "war on fat" is also an attempt to delineate symbolic boundaries between populations based on race and socio-economic status.)

Fat hatred pervaded the middle class as well. Historians like Hillel Schwartz and Peter N. Stearns trace the beginning of fat prejudice in the middle class to the development of consumer culture in the industrialized age. Members of the newly emerging middle class in the early to mid-twentieth century were being encouraged to consume—buy more products, engage in more leisure activities, be more beautiful, have more fun—in order to signal their success. This new hedonistic mindset was in direct conflict with the puritanical beliefs on which the country was founded—beliefs such as self-discipline, repression of impulses and desires, and denial of gratification that still undergird American discourse today. As a result, it became important to participate in consumer culture while still keeping up the appearance of self-control. As Farrell notes, "this cultural conflict got played out—and continues to get played out—on the body."

So the fat body became a sign of sloth, indulgence, primitivism, lack of control. A visible marker of inferiority. Over time, these beliefs were subsumed and adopted by the medical industry. In today's parlance, the fat body is evidence of an "epidemic." An indicator of disease, neglect. Depending on who you ask, the fat body is either a health problem that needs to be healed, or an eyesore that should be erased.

One need only glance through the comments section of an obesity-related article online for proof that fat people are still perceived by many as "not quite human." The anonymous comments that followed a 2012 article entitled "Donating Your Body to Science? Nobody Wants a Chubby Corpse" (the subject of which, I feel, is pretty self-evident) illustrate that fat hatred is alive and well, and extends beyond the grave:

**PO'd in MN:**
Donate it to Old Country Buffet. He must be the fat f--k that would always sit by me on the bus and take 3/4 of the seat. They take up too much space, are unpleasant to look at and cause global warming- yes, think how much fuel it takes to cart their fat a$$ around and transport their groceries. The extra material for clothes, etc. They are causing global warming. And now are clogging up the donation box at Corpse R Us. Oh, I know...must be a glandular thing.

**Not Falling For It:**
Not accepting of the 'live' fat ones either. Try mixing in the occasional salad!

**Airborn7:**
Well, speaking as a medical doctor, I don't want to see these porkers when they're alive. They are generally more prone to disease, they are all diabetic and will eventually get their renal failure or heart disease - in addition they have a much higher complication rate from even simple surgeries, and they can always find a sleaze bag attorney to sue for malpractice when anything goes wrong.

**ameridian:**
Listen up all fatties! There's a message here - "I'm fat and I'm proud" never did cut it. Not even after you're dead.

# Mommy

NORTH CAROLINA, APRIL–MAY 2010

```
PROGRESS NOTES          04/30/10          09:25

61 yo male s/p LRYGB. Admitted with septic shock due to
anastomosis leak. Leak persists, now s/p drainage of abscess
in VIR 4/24. Also with UGIB, s/p transfusion 9 units PRBC,
thought to be stress gastritis with bleeding from gastric
remnant.

Oxygen requirement increased overnight, now on 11 liters high
flow NC.
```

AT THE AGE of thirty-one, I thought I knew anger. I thought I had experienced it, expressed it, processed it, I thought I knew what it felt like. I am now learning anger anew.

Every morning my anger is a white heat seeping into my cereal; every evening I do yoga and drink. I find daily life unreasonable, unbearable. I am jerky movements, misdirected rage, a land mine in jeans. "Jennifer's life is *ruined*!" my mother tells strangers who will listen, her voice lightly laced with glee. When I push her in a wheelchair to the ICU, I want to slit her throat. I want to hate her. I want to hold her. Living with her is a terrible idea. I know this, I have known this, I will always know this. Now that she has recovered from her eye surgery, she is mad that I don't baby her enough. She wants to be waited on. She wants to be chauffeured, pushed in wheelchairs, cooked and cleaned for. She wants to be the one in the most pain. The sickest, the saddest, the most put-upon. She wanted all of this before our disaster began, but back then my father satisfied these needs for her. Now she expects me to fill his void.

She wants me to be her mommy. Well I want a mommy too, goddammit.

The only activity that weakens my anger is working out. I go to the gym early in the morning, and I often go to yoga at night. Every morning I beat up my body in lieu of beating my mother. She seems so supremely satisfied that the prophecy has come true—I have moved home to take care of her. I am living out my destiny, she believes. A daughter's job is to take care of her mother. She wants me to be her everything right now—her caretaker, her partner, her entertainment, her counselor, her maid, her cook, her parent. I can be none of those things. I call her primary care physician and ask her to refer my mother to a counselor, then I call the counselor's office and make the first appointment. It is the best I can do.

I have lunch with Ariane, an acquaintance from New York who happens to be visiting Durham. I almost cancel many times, but I don't. Since our family disaster began, I've been learning that people like to tell me that they "know how I feel." They like to give me advice. Their unsolicited advice and claims of kinship and understanding have started to piss me off even more than the powerlessness I feel every time I walk into the hospital. So I'm worried that Ariane is going to tell me what to do, or that she knows how I feel.

She does, and she doesn't. She tells me about what it was like to watch her mother die slowly at a young age from cancer. How it felt to be so young and take care of a parent. She gives me advice that's actually helpful. She says stuff like, "It's a marathon, not a sprint. Direction is everything. If things are moving in a positive direction, no matter how slow, that should give you hope. If things are only regressing, then you should prepare yourself." At the end of the lunch, she offers me a house. It's about ten minutes away from the hospital and will be unoccupied until June, when her father will arrive and take up residence in the house for the summer. I can stay in their house alone, for free, for a month.

I thank her very much for the offer, but turn it down. I can only imagine how angry and hurt my mother would be if I moved into a stranger's house and left her on her own. Plus, I will probably return to New York soon anyway. I don't know how much longer I can expect my employer to hold my job for me. I've got to find a way to extract myself from this situation soon, or I may never leave. On Friday, April 30 I write in my journal, "I think I'll stay one more week. Maybe go back to NY next weekend?"

The next morning I get up early and make some coffee before going to the gym. While I'm getting dressed, I hear my mother wailing, heaving, and moaning from her room. She calls to me, "Jennifer! Jennifer! Help me!" I rush in to find her sitting on the edge of the bed holding a small trash can in her lap, as if she is going to throw up. When I ask her what's wrong, she says, "The coffee. That smell is just terrible. I can't take it. I can't breathe." I turn the coffee machine off and pour the coffee down the sink. I go to the gym. I return an hour later and take a shower. As soon as I turn off the water and exit the shower, I hear my mother screaming. "Jennifer! Help! Help! Jennifer! I need you!" I wrap a towel around my body and rush into her room. She's on the edge of the bed again with the trash can. "I feel awful. Just awful. That coffee you made has made me so sick. I need to go to the emergency room." I tell her no, she probably doesn't need to go to the emergency room, and I need to go ahead and drive to Durham to check on Daddy.

As I'm getting dressed, my cell phone rings. It's the Durham ICU, calling to tell me that my father is in respiratory distress and they're going to have to intubate him again. Will I give consent for the procedure? From across the house, I can still hear my mother wailing and dry heaving into the trash can. I give consent for the procedure, then go tell my mother. She continues to insist that she needs to go to the emergency room. I say that I have to get to the ICU as soon as possible. While I'm finishing getting dressed, she calls 911 and requests an ambulance. The paramedics arrive as I'm getting ready to leave. I agree to follow the ambulance to the hospital and help her get checked in. On the way, I call Gail, my father's cousin who lives in Durham, and tell her what's going on. I ask if she can get over to the ICU as soon as possible to check on my dad. She says that she will.

At the Burlington hospital, I fill out all of the paperwork and go back to check on my mother. She's on a gurney, tucked underneath a white blanket. They've given her a small basin for her to vomit in, which she rests on her chest. I tell her that I'm sorry she doesn't feel well, but I need to get to Daddy. I can tell she's upset that I'm leaving her there alone, but I don't know what else to do.

My father is already intubated by the time I get to the ICU. His wrists are tied to the handrails of the bed. He fights against the restraints and tries to vomit out the tube that's down his throat. His eyes are bloodshot, watery, and partially open. I can see from his expression that he's in pain, and he's scared. I don't understand why he's not sedated, like he usually is when intubated. The doctor talks to me, but I don't fully process the information. She says something about taking a "major step back." I start to cry and shake. Gail tries to calm me down. My father keeps trying to vomit his intubation tube out, keeps trying to reach his arms up to pull it out.

My mother is discharged from the Burlington hospital later that day. They run some tests, but find nothing wrong. They give her some fluids and send her home.

A couple of days later I contact Ariane and tell her yes, I would very much like to take her up on her offer. I pack up my things and relocate to Durham.

# Gail

AT SOME POINT during the week after Easter Sunday, Gail appeared. Jack and I walked into the waiting room, and she was there. "Why didn't anybody call me?" she asked. One of my father's first cousins, Gail lived in Durham. I didn't think to contact her because, at the time, I barely knew her. And I had no idea that she lived in Durham.

Gail wears her short blonde hair in a fashionable bob, and her exquisitely sculpted eyebrows emphasize the same Blevins eyes that my father, brother, and I have. Big, beautiful, striking eyes that would compel nurses to declare, "You favor him! You really do favor him!" in thick Southern accents as I sat beside my father's hospital bed. Gail had had gastric bypass years earlier; she lost a great deal of weight, but eventually, like many gastric bypass patients, she gained part of it back.

Over the course of the next year, Gail would become an invaluable part of my life. She would invite me to live in her home, which was located a mere ten minutes from the hospital. She would listen to me vent about my mother, my father, my brother, my fears about my future. She would withhold judgment when I drank copious amounts of whiskey on the couch in her living room every night while we watched TV together. About the same age as my parents (and a mother herself), Gail would help me navigate the delicate business of becoming a parent to my parents.

She would ask nothing of me, during a time when circumstance was asking everything of me. She would make me laugh when I thought I had forgotten how. She would love, support, and care for me as if I were her daughter.

Early in the tragedy, my dear friend Kristin strategized with me about how to survive my situation. She advised me to "find the amulets"—to search for the hidden helpers along my path. Gail was one of my amulets—a bright, shiny gem in the midst of a profoundly shitty year.

# Findings Concerning for Leak

NORTH CAROLINA, APRIL 2010

EXAMINATION: 7350 - ABDOMEN 1 VIEW      Apr 28 2010

INDICATION: Followup [sic] anastomotic leak following gastric
bypass

...This study is limited by patient body habitus...This study
was initially performed as a preliminary to an upper GI study,
the patient refused the upper GI study.

TECHNICALLY, MY FATHER in his "altered mental state" told a nurse to go fuck herself
when she asked him to drink the contrast fluid, so his refusal of the upper GI study was
a little more forceful (and vulgar) than this report indicates.

The surgeons have decreed that I will be permitted to accompany him down to radiology for the tests. They know he's more likely to listen to me.

EXAMINATION: 7355 - UGI W/KUB (ALL PTS)      Apr 29 2010

REASON: CHECK FOR LEAK

IMPRESSION: Findings concerning for leak adjacent to the pigtail
catheter site, most likely at or near the gastrojejunostomy
site.

I go with him to the test. His body is so swollen today that his limbs are puffy like
marshmallows.

Once we're in radiology, a team of highly trained strangers transfers him from the
gurney to the exam table, sandwiching his body between the metal slab and the x-ray
machine. He screams from the pain. I put on a protective iron gown and then tip a

Dixie cup full of chalky liquid down his throat. The radiologist and I watch on the monitor as the black sludge travels down his esophagus and then spews out into his body. This is how the radiology report describes it: "Contrast fills the gastric pouch. Subsequently, contrast pools to the left of the pigtail catheter, extending superiorly and laterally. An additional trail of contrast extends toward the left medial diaphragmatic dome…The patient was unable to tolerate further imaging, and the exam was stopped at this point."

To me, the image looks like a squid releasing its ink into the ocean. Or like a broken pipe gushing oil into the Gulf of Mexico.

# SECTION THREE:

## Persistent Leak[s]

# Deepwater Horizon

GULF OF MEXICO, APRIL 2010

From *Report to the President: National Commission on the BP Deepwater Horizon Oil Spill and Offshore Drilling* (January 2011):

> BY THE TIME THE RIG CREW ACTED, GAS WAS ALREADY ABOVE THE BOP, ROCK-ETING UP THE RISER, AND EXPANDING RAPIDLY. AT THE COMMISSION'S NOVEM-BER 8, 2010, HEARING, A REPRESENTATIVE FROM TRANSOCEAN LIKENED IT TO "A 550-TON FREIGHT TRAIN HITTING THE RIG FLOOR," FOLLOWED BY WHAT HE DESCRIBED AS "A JET ENGINE'S WORTH OF GAS COMING OUT OF THE ROTARY." THE FLOW FROM THE WELL QUICKLY OVERWHELMED THE MUD-GAS SEPARATOR SYSTEM. IGNITION AND EXPLOSION WERE ALL BUT INEVITABLE. THE FIRST EXPLO-SION OCCURRED AT APPROXIMATELY 9:49 P.M.

NO ALARMS TO alert the rest of the (sleeping, showering, eating, Skyping) crew. One hundred twenty-six people on board: one hundred twenty men, six women. First, mud oozes out onto the rig floor. Then the crude, spattering and smothering and covering the drilling room and its men. The gas, invisible and silent, escapes and pervades, meets with a spark in the engines, and then

BOOM.

Black and smoke and mud and gas and blaze and blaze and death. Fragile bodies flung against steel walls. Crumbling infrastructure crunching bones. Blood and mud mingle, fire consumes flesh, and the dead disappear.

A blowout, a broken blowout preventer, a well 13,500 feet beneath the ocean floor. Unprecedented pressure pushing up through the well. A well performing its purpose: to give us oil. It gives us oil for eighty-seven days. Produces 210 million gallons of it. The Macondo well continues performing its purpose long after the Deepwater Horizon (paean of progress, exemplar of greed and need) burns into oblivion. A tower of fire. An unpluggable leak. A summer of spillage.

# Another Leak

## GULF OF MEXICO AND NORTH CAROLINA, APRIL 2010

AT FIRST I barely noticed it. A blazing platform in the middle of the ocean, surrounded by big boats shooting water at it. My father was on a different planet at the time, and I was up there with him—far above the workings of the world. It was just another calamity, a distant disaster, not nearly as important to me as my own. I must have seen images of it as I passed by the newspaper stands near the elevators on my way back to the ICU every morning. I probably paused on news coverage of it as I flipped through the channels on the TV in my father's room. There's no way I could have missed it. But it was in the background, like wallpaper or Muzak, so I didn't really pay attention to it. At least, not at first.

On April 20, 2010, the Deepwater Horizon oil rig exploded, killing eleven men and commencing the worst environmental disaster in US history. For two days after the explosion, a massive fire raged as an uncoordinated effort to put it out gradually and inadvertently sank the rig, thereby severing the connection between the Deepwater Horizon and the riser coming out of the 13,500-foot-deep Macondo well. Consequently, oil and gas began gushing out of the riser and into the surrounding water.

I knew very little about deepwater drilling when the disaster in the Gulf started; now I know that deepwater drilling is an elaborate, multistep process that involves the careful balancing of extreme pressures. As the workers aboard the rig drill into the ocean floor, inserting steel pipe as they go, they use a drilling fluid called "mud" as a weight to counter the pressure in the well and to prevent gas or water from coming up the pipe. The only things connecting the rig to the ocean floor are the riser (or drill pipe) and the blowout preventer (or BOP), which is the last line of defense against a well blowout. On April 20, 2010, the BOP failed to activate after multiple elements of the well failed. Highly combustible gas, drilling fluid, and oil surged out of the well like blood gushing out of a carotid artery. Engines exploded, people died, and, two days later, the rig sank.

Prior to April 20, 2010, the Deepwater Horizon was considered to be a top-of-the-line rig, the "rig [that] set the standard for all the others," because it could handle the most challenging jobs in a very risky business. Some oil industry experts have compared drilling wells in 5,000 to 10,000 feet of water to performing surgery at the bottom of the ocean. Similar to laparoscopic medical procedures, most of the work occurs remotely using computers and monitors, far from the actual site of the operation. Deepwater drilling is a highly ambitious and lucrative endeavor that requires great precision and skill. When successful, it could be viewed as an impressive example of man's ability to manipulate nature in service of his own ends. When unsuccessful, deepwater drilling can initiate a volatile conflict, pitting the technology of humans against the unpredictable power of nature.

In a press conference on May 2, twelve days after the explosion, President Obama said that "the most advanced technology available is being used to try and stop a leak that is more than 5,000 feet under the surface. Because this leak is unique and unprecedented, it could take many days to stop."

By that point, my father's leak was in about its sixth week (a necessary approximation, considering the fact that we were never able to pinpoint exactly when the leak began). I suppose that had I been aware of Obama's overly optimistic prediction on May 2, I might have found it humorous. But, then again, maybe not. Even though we were well over a month into our family disaster at that point, I still couldn't comprehend a leak like my father's, or the one in the Gulf, lasting for months. Back then I assumed that catastrophes contained themselves when certain breaking points had been reached. Now I consider my naïveté of that summer to be quite charming.

Around the time BP released the first underwater images of the leak on May 12, I started actively paying attention to the oil spill. Until I saw what it looked like, the leak wasn't real to me. Once BP began live streaming the leak on May 20 (after being pressured by Congress to release more information), footage from the "spill cam" played continuously in the upper corner of the screen on CNN as journalists, scientists, and BP and government officials shared conflicting accounts of the severity of the spill on a seemingly never-ending loop. From that point on, I kept the TV in my father's ICU room tuned to CNN most of the time.

I don't remember when I noticed the parallels between the two catastrophes. At the time, it was hard to see anything clearly, or to widen my perspective beyond what was right in front of me. But now it seems obvious: two leaks developed into two disasters that summer, as a body of water and the body of my father fought to survive the consequences of modern-day technological hubris. And all I could do was watch.

# The Stent, or Surgery #4

NORTH CAROLINA, MAY 2010

OPERATIVE REPORT

DATE OF SURGERY: 05/06/2010

INDICATION: Mr. Blevins is a 61-year-old male who underwent laparoscopic Roux-en-Y gastric bypass on March 24th. He was taken back to the operating room the following morning for some tachycardia which had initially been concerning for a leak. At the time of the operation, no leak was identified. However, there was a significant amount of old clot in the abdomen which was washed out. Mr. Blevins eventually did alright and was discharged from the hospital. However, approximately a week later [he] developed abdominal pain and was evaluated at another hospital. Eventually, he was transferred back to ————— Hospital and a leak at the gastrojejunostomy was confirmed. He has been in the intensive care unit for the last month on TPN with evidence of ongoing leak from the gastrojejunostomy. He is brought to the operating room today in hopes that we can stent across this leak and allow this to heal.

FINDINGS: Leak with well matured fistulous tract at site of the gastrojejunostomy.

THE DOCTORS KEEP him intubated for a week. While he's still intubated, they take him back to surgery to insert a stent, which they explain is sort of like a sheath that will let fluid pass freely past the site of the leak, giving the area time to heal. The surgeons seem optimistic. In the ICU staff's progress notes, one of the PAs writes, "Will discuss discontinuation of abx and starting of feeds with surgical team now that leak has been addressed and presumably resolved." I am not as optimistic.

I adjust to my new living space. The house Ariane has lent me is huge, classy, and comfy. I love the silence. No one yells for me, or at me. No TV blares nonsense at me. I love how clean and uncluttered the house is. Now that I have my own space, I start taking up more space. I let myself feel my feelings, let them expand and contract and overwhelm me. I realize that I am so very fucked—that *we* are so very fucked. I can't see a way out of this that doesn't end in my worst nightmare. One night while brushing my teeth, the full force of the last month hits me in one fell swoop, and I start to cry. I crumble to the yellow bath mat, letting my toothbrush fall to the floor. The crying is so intense that it becomes physically painful. My head hurts, my face hurts. I curl up in the fetal position and start to hyperventilate. I'm dizzy. I'm scared. I'm going to lose my father. I am going to watch him die.

I talk to my mother every day, usually more than once. Some days I drive to Burlington to pick her up and take her to the hospital. Other days she relies on Karen, the wonderfully kind woman who my parents pay to clean their house, to drive her to and from the hospital. Some days she doesn't come to the hospital at all. She is mad at me for moving—sulky, really. I feel guilty about it every time I see her, every time we talk on the phone. But I realize what she can't—that my act of self-preservation is for them. By taking care of myself, I will be better equipped to take care of them. I try to explain it, but she doesn't get it. She doesn't seem to believe in such things. I imagine she thinks it means I'm weak. Or selfish.

The day after the stent procedure, we have a "family meeting" with a couple of the members of my father's care team. It was my idea. I wanted to try to get a realistic, honest appraisal of his condition and predictions for the road ahead. My mother, Gail, and I sit down in a small conference room with one of the ICU physician assistants and one of Dr. Belfore's bariatric fellows. Right from the start, the meeting is a minor disaster. Each time the PA or surgical fellow begins talking, my mother interrupts them to bring up one of her own symptoms or medical conditions. She wants this meeting to be about how sick *she* is. She wants to be sicker than my father. Initially the PA and doctor look confused, then they start looking at me to intervene. Every time my mother stops talking, I try to get us back on task by asking a specific question about my father's condition. Finally, I am able to obtain the following information: (1) his kidneys are still not fully functional (and probably never will be), (2) it will likely take at least six to twelve months of hospital care before he will get to the point where he can rehabilitate, and (3) he will require aggressive rehab for at least another month or two at the end of that six- to twelve-month period before going home. There is also the possibility that he will never get to go home and will spend the rest of his life in a long-term care facility.

They extubate my father on May 8. It's the first day in about a month that I am actually able to have a conversation with him. He is alert and aware, but doesn't remember anything since his first surgery. I fill him in on everything. I'm so excited—I feel like my father is back, and now we can work together to blow all those depressing predictions out of the water. I tell him that he has a major battle ahead, but that I'll be beside him for it all. I say that I'll be his sidekick—I'll be Robin to his Batman, or Samwise Gamgee to his Frodo. He takes stock of all of the tubes coming out of him, all of the machines surrounding his bed, and the body that's too weak to move. Then he looks up at me and says, "Well, this isn't exactly what I had in mind."

The next day is Mother's Day. I pick up my mother in the morning and bring her to the hospital. We're both excited about the recent turn of events. She kisses and pets my father. She sits beside his bed and says, "Give me your paw." They hold hands as they talk. There's a sense of triumph and joy in the room. After our visit, I take my mother to Olive Garden for a Mother's Day lunch and give her a card. We get through the entire day without fighting.

# Surely They All Knew What They Were Doing, Didn't They?

GULF OF MEXICO, APRIL–MAY 2010

From *Report to the President: National Commission on the BP Deepwater Horizon Oil Spill and Offshore Drilling*:

THROUGHOUT THE FIRST MONTH OF THE SPILL, GOVERNMENT RESPONDERS OFFICIALLY ADHERED TO WHAT WE NOW KNOW WERE LOW AND INACCURATE ESTIMATES. NON-GOVERNMENTAL SCIENTISTS, ON THE OTHER HAND, USED THE SMALL AMOUNT OF PUBLICLY AVAILABLE FLOW DATA TO GENERATE ESTIMATES THAT HAVE PROVEN TO BE MUCH MORE ACCURATE.

SHORTLY AFTER THE Deepwater Horizon exploded and sank, the news of the leak went public. BP and government officials initially denied that oil was spilling into the Gulf. Rear Admiral Mary Landry, commander of the Eighth Coast Guard District, was the first to be put in charge of the federal government's response to the disaster. During her appearance on CBS's *Early Show* on April 23, Landry claimed, "At this time there is no crude emanating from that wellhead at the ocean floor…There is no oil emanating from the riser, either." This was not the first (nor the last) time that the public was lied to about the circumstances and scope of the spill.

The Deepwater Horizon disaster became a public relations nightmare for both BP and the Obama administration. Both made sure to emphasize and advertise their attempts to fix the leak. However, since all the approaches in the first couple of months failed, news reports of the Gulf disaster took on a farcical quality as the world watched the so-called experts fail time and time again, performing ineffectual procedures with funny names like "top kill" and "junk shot." As Joel Achenbach writes in *A Hole at the Bottom of the Sea: The Race to Kill the BP Oil Gusher*, "People would come to learn a guiding principle about Deepwater Horizon oil spill information: If it contained good news, it wasn't true."

On May 2, a few days before my father's first stent procedure, BP started drilling the first of two relief wells adjacent to the Macondo well. On May 7, the day after the stent surgery, they lowered a cofferdam, or containment dome, over the larger of the two leaks in the broken riser. (Shortly thereafter, they discovered a third leak.) Similar to my father's stent, the device was supposed to enable the safe passage of oil to a containment ship on the surface. However, this technique had been designed to work in shallower water, and the Macondo well was too deep. Gas combined with cold water to form hydrate crystals, which blocked the opening at the top of the dome. The procedure was a total failure.

One of the most upsetting (and frightening) aspects of the disaster in the Gulf was the fact that no one seemed to know what to do. Nobody had an adequate plan for addressing an oil spill in the ocean, even though deepwater drilling had been around for decades. It quickly became clear that BP was woefully unprepared to respond to a disaster of this magnitude. As Antonia Juhasz writes in *Black Tide: The Devastating Impact of the Gulf Oil Spill*, "This was the fourth-largest corporation on the planet, supported by the second-, the third-, and the fifth-largest corporations in the world, in turn supported by the wealthiest government the world has ever known. Surely they all knew what they were doing, didn't they? Surely they'd prepared for such an event, hadn't they?" When the top scientists and engineers working for some of the wealthiest and most powerful organizations in the world were at a loss, it started to look like the leak might possibly never get fixed—like human technological prowess was no match for the raw power of the natural world. After all, as rig worker Shane Roshto told his wife during his final visit home before dying in the Deepwater Horizon explosion, "Mother Nature just doesn't want to be drilled here."

# Do I Owe Anybody Anything?

NORTH CAROLINA, MAY 2010

EXAMINATION: 7355 - UGI W/KUB (ALL PTS)       May 17 2010

REASON: GASTROJEJUNOSTOMY LEAK

INDICATIONS: Status post gastric bypass surgery with gastrojejun-ostomy leak. Status post stent placement. Reevaluation for leak.

FINDINGS: Following administration of oral Gastrografin, contrast pools at the level of the stent. A small amount of contrast traverses through the stent, with most of the contrast extending to either side of the stent, consistent with leak.

ON MAY 17, my father and I make a trip down to radiology for another swallow study to check on the status of the stent. When we return to his ICU room, one of Dr. Belfore's fellows is waiting for me with a clipboard in her hand. Without offering any explanation, she asks me to sign a consent form for another surgical procedure. I tell her that I won't do it until someone explains to me what's going on. She says she doesn't know—Dr. Belfore just asked her to find me and get my signature. Finally, someone fills me in: the upper GI study showed that the stent has "migrated" from its original position and needs to be removed immediately before it moves any further. I sign the form, explain the situation to my father, and then go out to the waiting room, where Dr. Belfore is supposed to find me after the procedure.

She comes out about an hour or two later and sits down next to me. She tells me that she was able to remove the stent safely. I ask her why it moved, and she says that she doesn't know—sometimes that just happens. I ask her what we can do next. She pauses. "Well, we can wait for the leak to heal on its own and continue to feed and hydrate your father intravenously. Or we could perform another stent procedure." I ask her why a second stent procedure would be a good idea, given the fact that the first one failed. She sort of shrugs her shoulders and says something about it being the "only surgical option."

It's a terrifying moment. I feel like I'm falling, or standing at the bottom of a canyon alone. Next to me sits a highly regarded surgeon who teaches at a prestigious medical school, an expert in her field, and it's clear that she doesn't know what to do next. The challenges presented by my father's leak have exceeded her capabilities. The best option she can offer is to continue to deny my father food and water indefinitely, hoping that his body will solve the problem that she can't.

My father's mental status has been going downhill ever since that celebratory Mother's Day weekend. He's able to have simple conversations and participate in a little bit of physical therapy, but I have to constantly orient him and retell the saga of the last two months. He easily forgets where he is and why he's here. To help him, one of the ICU nurses makes a sign on bright yellow poster board that reads, "You are Jim Blevins. You are in the HOSPITAL. It is May," and hangs it on the wall by his bed.

The worst part is the fact that he keeps forgetting why he can't eat or drink. Some days he begs for food and water; other days, he tries new tactics. The day after the stent removal, he asks me to show him how to buy ice cream. I explain to him why he can't have any food, and I promise him that as soon as he can eat again I'll bring him any flavor of ice cream that he wants. He thinks about it for a while. He says, "Gin and tonic." "You want gin and tonic ice cream, Daddy?" I ask. He nods.

Later that same day, apropos of nothing, he turns to me and asks, "Do I owe anybody anything?" I tell him not to worry—that I'll take care of it if he does.

His pupils are tiny as pin points (a side effect of some of the pain medication, I'm told), and he has a faraway look in his eyes—as if he's mostly somewhere else. The sign on the wall says that he is Jim Blevins, but that's not entirely true. He's more like a child version of my father. He has the same personality, the same wit, but now he's simple and naïve, innocent and frightened. His world has shrunk to this room.

The ICU staff tells me that he's ready to be transferred to a surgical stepdown unit, but I'm skeptical. He's still entirely dependent on other people for all of his needs, and his mental status continues to deteriorate. He can't even sit up on the side of the bed without the assistance of a physical therapist, the therapist's assistant, and a nurse. But since the decision is not mine to make, the date of the transfer is set as May 20. On the morning of the transfer, various ICU staff members stop by his room to say goodbye. I snap a picture of my father lying in bed surrounded by five nurses and one of the PAs. They all look proud of him, as if he's graduating or something.

I pack up his things and bring them to his new room on the sixth floor in the bariatric wing, then come back downstairs to be with him for the transfer. They put the binder containing his chart on the bed between his legs, along with an oxygen canister that they connect him to after disconnecting him from the oxygen in the room, and a portable machine that checks his vital signs. The final step is to deflate the bed. At some point in April, they switched him to a special bed with a green, inflatable mattress that's supposed to prevent the formation of pressure ulcers. It's a very wide and spacious bed. Once they deflate the mattress, he has no cushion between his body and the metal base underneath.

We finally set out—a group of about five or six. I try to stay out of the way while also remaining close enough that he can see and hear me. They wheel his bed out of the ICU and into the elevator corridor. Someone pushes the button for the elevator. I reach down, squeeze his hand, and ask him how he's doing. He says that "this is all a little overwhelming," but he's "doing OK." Then the elevator doors open. When they go to push his bed into the elevator, they discover that it won't fit. The elevator is quite large and has been designed to transport patients in hospital beds, but it's not wide enough to accommodate his special bed. The nurses and aides try to get it to fit anyway. At first they are relatively gentle, but when their gentle methods fail they start shoving and jamming and banging the bed like it's a pinball machine in a dive bar. In the process, they forget the man in the bed.

As other staff members pass by, they stop and try to help solve the problem, so soon my father is surrounded by strangers who don't really see him. I watch as his already precarious sanity deteriorates. His eyes get wider. His forehead crinkles up. He pulls his blanket up higher and wraps his arms around his chest. He looks like a child who has been tucked into a public nightmare of being attacked by an angry mob. His eyes beg me to intervene, but I don't know how to stop the machine already in motion. I tell them that my father is getting upset and that their methods are clearly not working, but they keep banging the bed into the door frame. Finally, one of the nurses remembers that the bed width is adjustable. They adjust the bed to its narrower setting, and it slides into the elevator with ease. I squeeze in beside the head of the bed. As we travel up to the sixth floor, I check in with my father. Quiet and wide-eyed, he looks like he's in shock.

# On the Road

*3/23/86:*

*Today daddy taught me how to drive! And we had fun! And we got a drink yum! But daddy had to leave. bye!*

I REMEMBER THIS day. I was seven years old, and Ray had just turned six. As kids, we spent most of our time with Granny and my mother, so quality time spent with our father always felt special. On this day in 1986, he took Ray and me to Burger King for lunch and then drove us across the street to the empty parking lot of an abandoned shopping center. He took turns sitting us on his lap and letting us "drive" around the parking lot. For many years, I considered it to be one of the best days of my life.

So many of my early diary entries end with laments about my father going away, or celebrations about him coming home. He was in the National Guard (and later the Army Reserves), so in addition to working a full-time job, he was often gone on weekends. A few times he started new jobs in new cities without us, living in an apartment alone during the week and only coming home on weekends so that Ray and I could finish out the school year before moving to a new place. As a result, my childhood memories are dominated by Granny, Mommy, and Ray, with occasional Daddy punctuations. For some reason, a lot of those Daddy memories took place in cars.

When we were living in Charlotte, my father bought a brand-new 1990 Silver Oldsmobile Cutlass Ciera (the car that he would later let me take to college). Around this time, I wasn't particularly close to anyone in my family, and I felt isolated and alone. One day my father and I went out to run errands, just the two of us, and he turned up the radio so that I could check out the "great speakers" in the new car. We rode around for a while, not talking to each other. The George Michael song "One More Try" came on. It's a slow groove, sort of melancholy and elegiac. Every time the chorus kicks in, George sings about a "teacher" that he's afraid of loving. We listened to the song together in silence for a while, and the last time the chorus played my father said, "Why is that man singing about his T-shirt?" Like many of my father's jokes, it took me a minute. I started to laugh when I realized that he thought George Michael was saying "T-shirt," not "teacher." He added, "Must have been one hell of a T-shirt."

A few years later I sat behind the wheel of that Cutlass Ciera as my father taught me how to drive. He'd bring a mixed drink in a covered mug to sip on during our driving lessons, I think mostly because he enjoyed the irony. He sat in the passenger seat, cool and collected, drinking his bourbon while I swerved around tight corners and tailgated slow vehicles in front of us. Instead of screaming at me, or trying to take the wheel, he made smart-ass remarks like, "You know, I bet you could probably get closer to that car if you really tried. There's still a good inch or two left there to work with."

One of the only times I ever saw my father lose his temper happened in a different car about five years before the driving lessons. He had been laid off from his job earlier that year and hadn't been able to find another one. We were struggling financially, so he had started driving a run-down, old Plymouth Reliant. Our parents had been arguing a lot, and the energy in our home had been very tense for quite some time. One morning as my father was taking us to school, Ray and I started fighting about something stupid, as we often did. Daddy told us several times to cut it out, but we ignored him. Finally, he pulled into a parking lot, stopped the car, and started beating his head and hands against the steering wheel violently while screaming, "Shut up! Shut up! Just shut up, goddammit!" Ray and I were speechless…in total shock. We were used to such outbursts of anger from our mother, but never from our father. We rode the rest of the way to school in silence. I think that may have been the first time that I became aware of the fact that my father was human—that he was emotional and fragile just like the rest of us.

# Moving, Part One

NORTH CAROLINA, MAY 2010

*5/20/10: Moved to [room] 6312. The move traumatized him—they couldn't fit the bed into the elevator and it became quite a circus. Poor Daddy.*

*He's very obsessed with horses today.*

ONCE THEY GET him into his new room, they inflate the mattress and connect him to the oxygen source in the wall and the room's vital signs monitor. Amber, the night nurse, stops in to introduce herself. I tell her about the elevator incident. I warn her that he's had twenty-four-hour, intensive attention and care for the last six weeks, so he's probably going to occupy a great deal of her time tonight. She assures me that she can handle it. "Nursing is my calling," she says in a thick Southern accent. "God called me to nursing, and I feel like I'm doing God's work taking care of people. Don't worry, honey. Your daddy's in good hands."

I've been in the hospital since 9 a.m.; it's now about 7 p.m., and I'm tired and hungry. I don't want to leave, though, until I feel like he has adjusted to his new surroundings. He doesn't look like the same man who greeted me this morning in the ICU. He has a sort of wild look in his eyes. I sit with him and try to calm him down.

(*A dimly lit hospital room. FATHER lies in hospital bed; JENNIFER sits in chair beside bed.*)

FATHER:   I have some…concerns.

JENNIFER:  OK, Daddy. What are your concerns?

FATHER:   I want to talk about horses.

JENNIFER:  OK, let's talk about horses. What do you want to say about horses?

FATHER:   I am in a hospital for horses. Am I a horse?

JENNIFER:     No, Daddy, this is a hospital for human beings, and you are a human being.

FATHER:       If the physicians in this hospital are trained to treat horses, how are they also able to treat human beings?

JENNIFER:     The physicians in this hospital are trained to treat human beings, of which you are one.

FATHER:       Are you sure?

JENNIFER:     Yes, I am sure that you are a human being and that the doctors in this hospital have been trained to treat you, not horses.

FATHER:       What about…shoes?

JENNIFER:     No, you are not a shoe. The physicians in this hospital *wear* shoes, but they are not trained to *treat* shoes.

FATHER:       I see. (*pause*) I'm scared.

JENNIFER:     I know, Daddy. I'm sorry. It's going to be OK. I'm going to go home in a few minutes, but I'll be back first thing in the morning.

FATHER:       I've never died in this world before.

JENNIFER:     (*pause*) No, you haven't. Do you think you're going to die, Daddy?

FATHER:       How do I get from my world to your world? (*gestures moving from his position to her position with his hand*)

JENNIFER:     We're in the same world, Daddy. We're both in the same room in the same hospital.

FATHER:       Please feed me.

JENNIFER:     Oh Daddy, I wish I could. You have no idea how badly I want to feed you.

FATHER:     (*pause*) Maybe I'll just stop at this point. What do you think?

JENNIFER:   Do you mean stop trying to get better?

            (*He nods.*)

JENNIFER:   Do you want to stop?

            (*He nods.*)

JENNIFER:   (*pause*) Well, that would be a shame, after everything you've already been through. I think we should keep going. Don't you?

FATHER:     Keep going?

JENNIFER:   Yeah, let's just keep going. Might as well. I mean, we've come this far, right?

FATHER:     Right.

JENNIFER:   So let's keep going a little while longer. OK?

FATHER:     Yeah.

I say goodnight, give him a kiss, and tuck him in. On my way out, I locate Amber and give her my cell number. I reiterate that he's probably going to need a lot of attention tonight, and Amber again reassures me that I have no cause to worry. I go home, eat some leftovers, drink some whiskey, and pass out.

My cell phone rings at 12:45 a.m. It's Amber. "Your father is out of control," she tells me. "He's going on and on about some conspiracy theory, he keeps trying to tear his lines out, and I just don't have time to deal with it. I mean, I *do* have other patients, you know!" She asks me to come back to the hospital and sit with him until the morning shift arrives, at which point they'll start having a "sitter" stay in his room twenty-four hours a day to watch him, she says. Apparently Amber's divinely ordained powers of healing only apply to sane, obedient patients.

I roll out of bed, put some clothes on, and drive back to the hospital. I have to enter through the ER because all of the other entrances are locked. As soon as I walk in his room, I can see that my father is totally wired. They've given him a dose of Ativan to calm him down, but it has only revved him up. He's so relieved I'm here, he tells me, because there are people after him and we need to get out of here as soon as possible. I sit down next to the bed and ask him who these people are. He can't tell me, he says. He's not really sure. But we need to leave <u>RIGHT</u> <u>NOW</u>.

The rest of the night is chaotic, exhausting, and occasionally comical. Every time I think I've successfully calmed him down and I can finally get some sleep in the recliner next to his bed, he starts cutting a shine. Sometimes he tries to pull the various lines out of his arms. Sometimes he starts yelling, "Help! Help! Police officer! Help!" Sometimes he does both. Whenever I catch him trying to pull out one of his lines, his facial expression is like that of a small child caught misbehaving. He knows he's being bad, and it seems like he's kind of enjoying it. He'll wait until I've contorted my body into a semi-comfortable sleeping position in the recliner, covered myself with the blanket, and started to drift off to sleep. Then he'll yell, or yank his lines, or fight with the bed rails and try to roll out of the bed. It pisses me off, but at one point the situation strikes me as being really fucking funny. I laugh, which makes him laugh. "Daddy, is this payback for keeping you up at night when I was a baby?" I ask. He responds by trying to yank his IV out again.

Neither one of us sleeps a wink all night.

# Moving, Part Two

May 27, 2010

Jennifer Blevins

_____ 72nd Street, #E3

Brooklyn, NY 11209

Michael _____

_____ Street

Brooklyn, NY 11220

Re: --- 72nd Street, Apt. E3, Brooklyn, New York 11209

Dear Michael:

I will be vacating the above referenced premises on June 7, 2010. Verbal notice was given over the phone on May 22, 2010. I will leave the premises in "broom clean condition." I will leave the key to the front door of the building and the mailbox key next to the sink, and the key to the door of the apartment in the #E3 mailbox; the lock on the mailbox has been broken the entire time I have resided in #E3, so I can just open the door without the key.

Please do not enter the premises until after I have vacated on June 7, 2010. To confirm in writing what I communicated to you during a phone call in early April and a phone call on May 22, 2010: I am vacating the premises because my father has been severely ill and in the intensive care unit of a hospital in North Carolina for almost two months. I am leaving New York to come down to North Carolina to take care of my father. If these were not the circumstances, I would not be vacating the apartment.

Sincerely,

Jennifer Blevins

# I Would Like My Life Back

## NORTH CAROLINA, MAY 2010

*5/22/2010: He asked me what I want to dream about tonight. I said adventures; he said aliens.*

AROUND THE TIME of the elevator incident, I made the decision to officially quit my job and relocate to North Carolina on a long-term temporary basis. I was tired of living in limbo, and it had become clear to me that my father's medical saga was still only just beginning. I was apprehensive about this decision for many reasons.

First, I worried that I might never live in New York again. I loved living there and I wasn't ready to leave. Also, I was concerned that if I ever did return to New York, I wouldn't be able to find another job that I actually wanted to work, which would force me to return to my old pattern of working miserable monkey jobs to support myself. Of course, there was also the possibility that I wouldn't even be able to *find* a job, monkey or otherwise. By relocating to North Carolina, I also ran the risk of my parents becoming so dependent on me that I would never be able to extricate myself from the situation. I had always assumed that I would end up caring for my parents at some point, but I never thought that I would have to begin doing so when I was only thirty-one years old and they were only sixty-one.

Additionally, my decision meant becoming financially dependent on my parents (well, technically my mother, since my father was on another planet), as I felt like it would be impossible to secure and retain a new job in Durham while also being the primary person in charge of my father's care and remaining on-call for my mother's various needs. I knew from a lifetime of experience that my mother attached conditions to money and gifts; oftentimes when I received either from her, I was expected to agree with her, be "nice to her," and do anything she said. But more so than the fear of my mother's conditions, I just really hated the idea of having to take money from my parents. I knew that they didn't have a lot of it.

Moving to North Carolina meant giving up my independence and my life in New York, so it was a decision that I did not make lightly. One development that made the decision a little easier, however, was Gail's offer to let me move in with her. During our time spent at the hospital together, I was growing to love Gail, and I could tell that we would get along well as roommates. Her house was only about ten minutes from the hospital, so I could continue to be close enough to rush over for emergencies when necessary.

As unnerving as it was, I felt good about my decision. The thought of going back to New York while my father was in such a helpless state hurt my heart. My mother had started growing more independent since I moved out in early May—sometimes even driving herself to the hospital—but I knew that she still needed me close by. Ray had been calling regularly to check in, and he came down for a visit the weekend after we moved into the new room. When I told him about my decision to move I could tell that he felt bad about it, and I tried to reassure him. Given the fact that the burden of helping our parents had mostly fallen to him in the years while I had been living in New York, it actually felt kind of good to be able to spare him from the full brunt of this new hell. Also, I feared that if I didn't move to North Carolina and continue the work I'd been doing since Easter, I might not have a family to come home to by Christmas.

So, while my father ranted and raved at the History Channel, I sat in the recliner by his bed with my laptop, a notebook, and my phone and planned my move. I booked a ticket on a flight to LaGuardia on May 31 with a return flight on June 7, giving me a week to wrap up my New York life. I reserved a storage unit in Brooklyn, where I would move most of my belongings. (I figured that I would be much more likely to return to New York if most of my possessions were still there.) I reserved a couple of movers to take my stuff from the apartment to the storage unit. I called my boss and quit my job, thanking him profusely for his incredible patience with my situation. I called my landlord and informed him that I had to break the lease on my apartment; he was unreasonably nasty, telling me that I was making a big mistake because my father was "probably going to die anyway" and that if I broke my lease I would "have a hard time finding another apartment" because he might not give me a good reference. New York City landlords are a unique breed of asshole.

On May 30, the day before I flew back to New York to pack up my apartment and officially relocate to Durham indefinitely, Tony Hayward, the CEO of BP, was asked by reporters what he would say to the people in Louisiana who were starting to see oil wash up on their beaches from the still-gushing leak in the Gulf. In one of his biggest gaffes, Hayward responded by saying, "We're sorry for the massive disruption it's caused their lives. There's no one who wants this over more than I do. I would like my life back." When I heard that I thought, "Ha. You and me both, Tony." But I had a feeling that my father wanted his life back even more than I did. And I imagined that the eleven men who died in the Deepwater Horizon explosion would have probably liked theirs back, too.

# Just Like a Crime Scene

## GULF OF MEXICO, MAY 2010

From a BP press release:

> UPDATE ON GULF OF MEXICO OIL SPILL - 29 MAY
> RELEASE DATE: 28 MAY 2010
>
> BP STARTED THE "TOP KILL" OPERATIONS TO STOP THE FLOW OF OIL FROM THE MC252 WELL IN THE GULF OF MEXICO AT 1300 CDT ON MAY 26, 2010.
>
> THE PROCEDURE WAS INTENDED TO STEM THE FLOW OF OIL AND GAS AND ULTIMATELY KILL THE WELL BY INJECTING HEAVY DRILLING FLUIDS THROUGH THE BLOW-OUT PRE-VENTER ON THE SEABED, DOWN INTO THE WELL.
>
> DESPITE SUCCESSFULLY PUMPING A TOTAL OF OVER 30,000 BARRELS OF HEAVY MUD, IN THREE ATTEMPTS AT RATES OF UP TO 80 BARRELS A MINUTE, AND DEPLOYING A WIDE RANGE OF DIFFERENT BRIDGING MATERIALS, THE OPERATION DID NOT OVERCOME THE FLOW FROM THE WELL.
>
> THE GOVERNMENT, TOGETHER WITH BP, HAVE THEREFORE DECIDED TO MOVE TO THE NEXT STEP IN THE SUBSEA OPERATIONS, THE DEPLOYMENT OF THE LOWER MARINE RISER PACKAGE (LMRP) CAP CONTAINMENT SYSTEM. . .
>
> THIS OPERATION HAS NOT BEEN PREVIOUSLY CARRIED OUT IN 5,000 FEET OF WATER AND THE SUCCESSFUL DEPLOYMENT OF THE CONTAINMENT SYSTEM CANNOT BE ASSURED.

As I WAS preparing for my trip to New York, BP tried again to stop the leak. The "top kill" consisted of three days of pumping drilling mud down into the well to counter-act the pressure of the oil rising up, and the "junk shot" technique involved injecting objects like golf balls and pieces of rubber into the well to stop its flow. Once again, BP failed.

It was around this time that the federal government started becoming more actively involved in the decision-making process. However, it remained clear that neither BP nor the federal government was prepared to contend with a well blowout and oil spill of such magnitude (and, as a congressional hearing on June 15 revealed, nor were any of the other major oil companies). In the months and years that followed the spill, investigations would reveal that BP's culture of greed and endemic corner cutting were responsible for the disaster, and that same culture was pervasive throughout the oil industry. Additionally, some of the government officials working for the federal agency charged with monitoring the oil industry were literally in bed with it. In 2008, the inspector general of the Minerals Management Service, the governmental agency in charge of collecting oil and gas royalties at that time, reported to Congress that current and former members of the agency were suspected of "financial self-dealing, accepting gifts from energy companies, cocaine use and sexual misconduct." The incestuous relationship between the oil industry and the government extends beyond gifts, sex, and coke—offshore drilling leases are the second largest source of income for the US Treasury.

With initially very little governmental oversight, BP was put in charge of the containment and cleanup of the most significant environmental disaster in US history—that it had caused—because there seemed to be no other alternative. When a local resident tried to volunteer for BP during the cleanup effort, he was presented a contract with a confidentiality clause. Later he recalled, "I realized that it was just like a crime scene… They killed our Gulf, and now the murderer is in charge of cleaning up the scene of the crime."

# I Am a Sunni God

NORTH CAROLINA, MAY 2010

*5/25/2010: Very agitated and angry. Screaming and yelling. Watched Star Trek: The Next Generation all day.*

MY FATHER'S "ALTERED mental status" is becoming more altered. He's argumentative and combative. Also, he is incredibly anemic. They can't keep his blood count up; they've been transfusing up to two or three bags of blood a day, to no avail. I feel like we're not always receiving all of the information about my father's condition, but I have no way of proving this. I'm getting very anxious about leaving here for a week. So is my mother.

She and I put together a list of issues to discuss with Dr. Belfore the next time we can corner her:

1) Why is his blood count down?
2) Can we put him back on Cardizem [a heart medication] and back in CCU?
3) Can the stent (size, type, etc.) be changed?
4) We do not want him to leave this hospital with this leak.
5) Why can't you devise a way to surgically fix the leak?
6) DNR for heart attack.

My mother and I have decided to change his code status to DNR (do not resuscitate) in the event of a heart attack. For now, they are still supposed to intubate him if he goes into respiratory distress again. We may alter that instruction in the future.

In the morning, Dr. Belfore and her fellows (who my mother and I have started refer-ring to as her "minions") come into the room during their rounds. They surround the bed and discuss his condition. My father's eyes are glazed and unfocused, and he mumbles incoherently to himself. Dr. Belfore addresses him by saying, "Good morn-ing. Could you tell us who you are, please?" He nods his head. "I am a Sunni god," he says. I watch the surgeons struggle to suppress their laughter, a white-coated mass of contorted mouths. I enjoy their discomfort.

On her way out, I ask Dr. Belfore if she can come back this afternoon after my mother gets to the hospital so that we can meet with her to discuss the plan for moving forward. She says that she will try to stop by.

Throughout the day, my father argues with me, the television, and anyone who walks in the room. Since I'm the one he's around the most, I receive the worst of it. He says things like, "You're a terrible disappointment as a daughter," and "You're killing me. Please. You're ruining everything!" As the day wears on, he begins to lament his condition. "Why me?" he cries. "Why would someone put me through this hell?" In a rare moment of lucidity around lunchtime (which, of course, he cannot eat), he turns to me and says, "I promise I'll make this up to you." I tell him that's not necessary, but I appreciate the sentiment.

I keep *Star Trek: The Next Generation* on the TV all day. It's a show we both love and used to watch together when I was growing up. I hope that it might be soothing or therapeutic for him (and at least it gives us a break from the damn History Channel). But even the dulcet sound of Patrick Stewart's voice isn't enough to calm my father down.

My mother drives herself to the hospital, and I meet her downstairs with a wheelchair to help her to the room. When Dr. Belfore arrives, the three of us step out into the hallway to talk. I bring the wheelchair with us so that my mother can sit down while we meet. Since we're in the bariatric wing of the hospital, various post-surgical fat patients in hospital gowns and sticky socks slowly walk up and down the hall, pushing their IV poles beside them. Dr. Belfore casually leans against the wall in her scrubs, her curly russet hair tucked beneath a blue surgical cap.

I start running through my list of questions and concerns, but Dr. Belfore is distracted and aloof. She keeps checking her pager and her watch. She says things like, "You should begin thinking about long-term care," and "I've sent patients home with feeding tubes before. It has been done." I'm a little shocked and don't quite know how to respond. My father is currently a raging lunatic who cannot drink, eat, walk, or sit up on the edge of the bed (or even participate in physical therapy, because he can't follow commands or have a sane conversation), his blood count plummets to the point where they have to give him two or three bags of blood a day, and the leak in his digestive system is still not fixed…and his surgeon is talking about sending him home?

Everything about our conversation, from her body language to her dismissal of my concerns, communicates to me that she has reached the point where she is just trying to get rid of us. This skinny little woman standing beside me, who performed the very surgery that got us into this nightmare to begin with, seems to have decided that she has done all she can for us and it's time for her (and us) to move on. Oh *hell* no. I hear my father yelling in the room behind us, and I feel the anger I usually try to suppress during my encounters with Dr. Belfore boiling up in me. I stop her mid-sentence and say, "We are not leaving this hospital until you fix this leak." She tries to explain that "it's more complicated than that." I say again, "Two months ago my father was a fully functioning human being. We are not leaving this hospital until you fix him." My mother echoes my concern; finally she and I have found something we can agree on.

I've had people ask me why we don't go to another hospital and find another surgeon. Those people really don't seem to get it. First of all, just moving my father to another *floor* in the same hospital is a difficult, traumatic experience, let alone transferring him to another hospital in another city. Secondly, where would we go? Where would we find a more qualified and experienced bariatric surgeon (who will also take my father's health insurance) within the state of North Carolina? This is a surgeon who teaches other surgeons how to perform bariatric surgery at one of the best medical schools in the country—what other option do we have? Similar to the people in the Gulf affected by the oil spill, my mother and I feel that we have no choice but to trust the same person who surgically initiated our disaster to fix it.

# Surgery #5: The Stomach Was Freed, or The Big One

NEW YORK AND NORTH CAROLINA, JUNE 2010

OPERATIVE REPORT

DATE OF SURGERY: 06/03/2010

PREOPERATIVE DIAGNOSIS: Gastric bleed in the remnant stomach, also a GJ leak.

POSTOPERATIVE DIAGNOSIS: Gastric bleed in the remnant stomach, also a GJ leak with a perforated gastric remnant ulcer and bleed.

ESTIMATED BLOOD LOSS: 2200 mL

DESCRIPTION OF PROCEDURE: After informed consent was obtained, the patient was already in the operating room from [his] previous EGD that was being performed through his port that had been placed through the old G-tube site, so we had converted to open. We began by making an upper midline incision carrying this down to the level of the fascia and carefully went through the fascia using electrocautery and sharp dissection until we got into the peritoneal cavity. The bowel from underneath the peritoneal cavity was densely adherent to the upper layer, so a meticulous dissection was done with sharp dissection and electrocautery in order to free up the superior Roux limb and the gastric remnant in the left upper quadrant of the abdomen. This took greater than 85 minutes of extensive lysis of adhesions of adhesions. Once this was done, we were able to place the Thompson retractor into the abdomen and retract out of our way the sides of the abdominal wall...

The stomach was freed and was passed posteriorly to the Roux limb and pulled over to the right side of the abdomen...

There was a mass within the stomach that correlated with where the ulceration at the superior aspect of the remnant and stomach was...

In the posterior aspect of the Roux limb, there was a hole that had positive air bubbles coming out upon inspection. We then repaired this hole...

We used a Seldinger technique to place [a drainage tube] in the right mid abdomen without difficulty suturing circumferentially the small bowel up to the abdominal wall just below the entry site of the tube. Once this was done, we then closed the abdominal fascia using looped 1 Maxon suture and the skin was closed after copious irrigation with the staples. Dr. Belfore was present for the entirety of the case. All lap, sponge and instrument counts were correct at the end of the case. No other pathology was noted within the abdominal cavity upon exiting the case.

BEING BACK IN New York felt surreal. The city and its inhabitants grinded on as if nothing had happened. As if the entire world hadn't changed. Most of the advertisements in the subway stations and trains were the same ones I had stared at while commuting to my job on the Upper East Side just two months earlier. My apartment was identical to how I had left it—small, sparsely furnished, a little lonely. The weather was gorgeous. The first week of June in New York is almost always sunny and pleasantly warm, with azure skies and marshmallow clouds. It's an excellent time to visit.

Except I wasn't visiting New York, of course; I had come there to leave her. The night I arrived, Jack came over and we had pizza and beer. Two of our mutual friends, Dasha and Sonora, had generously ordered an array of boxes and packing materials to be delivered to my apartment; Jack and I crawled into one of the biggest boxes together and snapped some selfies. In the days that followed, I took breaks from packing up my apartment for various lunch and dinner dates with friends to whom I wanted to say goodbye. I took solitary walks around places like the East Village, the Upper West Side, my neighborhood in Brooklyn. When riding a subway train over the East River, I'd stare at the Statue of Liberty for as long as she was in view. "Hey there, pretty lady," I would whisper under my breath. "Bring me back," I'd ask.

The situation in North Carolina was getting worse every day, but there was nothing I could do but keep packing my apartment and hope my father didn't die during my absence. Dr. Belfore finally admitted that my father needed more surgical intervention. They determined that his blood count kept dropping because of a bleeding ulcer in his remnant stomach. Initially they tried inserting a drainage tube through the abdomen and into the remnant stomach, but nothing would drain. Then, on June 3, they took him into surgery (his fifth at that point) for what was intended to be a laparoscopic procedure to repair the remnant stomach. However, once they got inside his abdomen they discovered that the remnant stomach was, according to the surgical report, "completely full of clotted blood." At first they tried to repair it, but then they made the decision to remove it entirely. At that point they switched to an "open" procedure, wherein they gutted him like a fish and "freed" his stomach, leaving him only the tiny stomach pouch that had been created during the initial gastric bypass (which was still leaking, and therefore not fully functional). It was the most invasive surgery yet.

On June 3 as I was packing up the contents of my desk, I received a call at 1 p.m. from Dr. C., my favorite of Dr. Belfore's minions. He was by far the most human. (I was learning that someone like Dr. C.—a surgeon who had excellent interpersonal communication skills and a strong sense of compassion—was a rarity.) He told me that my father was still in surgery, and that they had discovered the remnant stomach was too damaged to repair, so they would have to open him up and remove it. There was no other viable option. He described the procedure and listed the potential risks, which included death. They had not succeeded in contacting my mother, so would I give consent for the procedure? I said yes. Dr. C. asked a nurse to get on the line with us to serve as a witness. Once she was on, he asked, "Will you please identify yourself?" "I am Jennifer Blevins, daughter of James Ray Blevins." "Do you consent to the open removal of your father's remnant stomach?" he asked. "Yes, I consent."

After I hung up, I stared out my apartment window at the beautiful day. My body was charged with fear and nervous energy, which made me start to shake a little. I felt compelled to do something—anything, but there was nothing I could do that would help my father. So I decided to go to the gym. I went online and signed up for a barre class in Manhattan, changed my clothes, grabbed my purse, and left my apartment. As soon as I got down to the street, I pulled my iPod out of my purse and changed the setting to shuffle. Immediately George Michael's "Faith" started to play, and I smiled. I decided that George was right—I gotta have faith.

That workout ended up being one of the best of my life. I channeled all of the fear and energy coursing through my body and gave it something to do. I thought about my father's weak, mutilated body, and I imagined sending it some of my strength. I thought of my mother's frail, sick body, and I envisioned sending it strength, too. I recommitted myself to the decision I had made and tried to have faith that I was strong enough to handle whatever was going to happen as a result of that surgery. *But he isn't going to die today*, I determined. *George Michael said so.* Fortunately George, my new spirit guide, was right.

The next day, BP made another attempt to stop the flow of oil in the Gulf by lowering another containment dome known as a "lower marine riser package," or LMRP, over the leaking riser. While it didn't stop the leak, it did start capturing about 25,000 barrels of oil a day. It was the first sign of success in the battle to stop the flow of oil into the Gulf. It made me wonder if our disaster was about to turn a corner, too.

The movers arrived on June 6. Jack came over to offer moral support. After we watched the movers cram my stuff into a seven-by-eight-foot storage unit, we went back to his place, where I spent the night. The next morning at the airport, I wrote in my journal: "Sitting in LGA, flight to RDU is delayed. 90% of my material possessions are in unit 8219 of the 41 Flatbush Ave storage unit. I am a nomad. I have no idea what happens next."

# Coin Toss

NORTH CAROLINA, JUNE 2010

CONSULTATION REPORT

DATE OF CONSULTATION: 06/08/2010

REASON FOR CONSULTATION: Evaluate patient with recent gastric leak repair, evaluate for antibiotic management.

The patient is considerably weaker than he was 7-10 days ago per his daughter. He answers some questions appropriately, but quickly drifts back to sleep. The patient does complain of some abdominal pain. He denies any shortness of breath. He denies any nausea or vomiting. The patient is unable to provide any other significant review of systems at [the] time of this evaluation.

I RETURN TO North Carolina and move in with Gail. She basically gives me the run of the second floor in her cozy two-story house. From what I have gathered thus far, since retiring from a career in human resources a couple of years ago, Gail has devoted most of her time to the following obsessions: QVC, autopsy shows, *Ancient Aliens*, *Ghost Hunters*, and working out at Curves. Her house is full of products she bought from QVC, and in her kitchen cupboards I regularly come across food products that expired two to five years ago. Gail's laid-back attitude and sharp wit make me feel at home from day one.

I return to the hospital. My father's status is once again considered "critical," so he's back in the ICU. Walking down the hall of the ICU feels like Old Home Week. Nurses, nursing assistants, respiratory therapists, physical therapists, doctors—they all take a moment to acknowledge my return. Some stop and talk to me, telling me how sorry they were to see my father back in the ICU. Some say they've been asking about me, wondering where I was. Some just nod sympathetically to me as I walk by. I know every person I pass.

My father is in a different room this time. It's small and hot. I see the long, thick incision down the center of his stomach for the first time; it's about eight to ten inches long, and I watch as a nurse puts a wound vac (vacuum dressing) over it to make it heal faster. During the surgery, the doctors also inserted a feeding tube that goes directly into his intestines, which hopefully means he'll get more nutrition than he's been receiving through the TPN that's administered through his arm.

He drifts in and out of consciousness. The fierce insanity of late May is gone; now he can barely keep his eyes open. It is the weakest I've ever seen him. I think he recognizes me and knows that I'm here next to him, but I can't be sure.

I have a conversation with the ICU doctor in charge of his care. He says that my father's fate is "a coin toss right now," and the coming weeks will likely determine whether he will one day be able to return to a normal life, or will require "long-term chronic care" for the rest of his life.

Over the next few days, my mother, Gail, and I discuss how to proceed. He's been through such hell, and we don't know how much more to put him through. At what point does it become cruel to consent to these procedures and prolong his suffering? My mother and I add another caveat to his DNR: we will consent to intubation only if it will be a short course. Being intubated is clearly miserable and traumatic for him, and we really don't want to put him through that experience again.

One of the biggest unknowns is his mental status. Has this experience permanently affected his brain, or is the doctors' hypothesis correct—will his mind return to normal once he's not critically ill? From the living will I found, and from various conversations I've had with my father, I know that he would not want his life prolonged if his mental abilities were permanently compromised. But the problem is, at what point will we know if they have been?

It's a very tense, emotional week. Every day his breathing becomes more labored and he has more difficulty opening his eyes. The doctors tell us that his lungs have simply grown too weak to support his body. They suggest a tracheostomy, which is what we've been trying to avoid. My fear is that once he goes on a ventilator, he will never get off of it.

I call Stacy, my doctor friend from college, who has been my unofficial medical consultant since the near-fatal Easter weekend. I fill her in on his condition and present my dilemma. Stacy is a radiation oncologist, so she deals with dying patients often. During our conversation, she offers two crucial pieces of advice. The first: "Blev, whatever decision you make will be the right decision. You have to believe that whatever you end up doing, it was the right thing to do." Then she says, "But you may want to consider this: if you decide not to go ahead with the trach, then *you* are the one making the decision to give up. If he gets the trach he may still give up, but if he does then *he* will be the one deciding to give up—not you."

# Respiratory Status Very Tenuous

NORTH CAROLINA, JUNE 2010

PROGRESS NOTES:              06/11/10              11:47

61 yo male s/p LRYGB, initial admission for septic shock
secondary to anastoamosis [sic] leak. Complicated by [acute
renal failure] requiring HD, a fib with RVR, and fungemia.
Also with GI bleed from gastric remnant, G-J stent ultimately
placed for leak, was displaced then removed. Pt to stepdown,
initially did well, however ultimately developed another GI
bleed. 6/3 had resection of bleeding gastric remnant, repair
of G-J leak, and placement of J tube. Was transfused a total
of 30 units of blood.

Did not sleep overnight, now up to 7 L NC, tachypnea, still with
AMS.

Neuro: does not follow commands...

Resp: Respiratory fatigue, desats with minimal movement,
respiratory status very tenuous. Have discussed possibility
of trach and slow vent wean with pts daughter and Dr. Belfore,
think this would give us the best [chance] of being able to
rehab pt. Family will consider options.


ON THE EVENING of Friday, June 11, my father's oxygen saturation kept dropping
throughout the night. The ICU claims that they tried calling me, but I never received
a call or a message. When I arrive on Saturday morning, he's gasping for air and his
oxygen saturation is in the low 80s. Today's the day when we have to decide.

His room is so hot, so close. The machines and furniture crowd the available space,
leaving little room for humans. I sit next to him and try to wake him up by speaking
loudly into his ear and grabbing his hand. I want him to tell me what to do. My mother
and Gail arrive. The three of us sit in the overheated, overcrowded room and watch him

struggle to breathe. My mother sits next to him, crying and holding his hand, while I stand on the other side of the bed. She looks up at me and says, "Oh Jennie, what should we do? Tell me what to do, Jennie. I don't know what to do." She cries harder. I step out into the hall and call Ray. I tell him that we've reached the point where we need to make a decision. He pauses, takes a breath. "You're the agent in the field," he says. "You decide."

I come back into the room and take a long look, searing the scene into my memory: My mother is wearing a pink shirt, Gail's wearing a gray one, and I'm wearing blue. The sun accosts us through the room's small window. My father has an oxygen mask over his face. His head lolls. He tries to open his eyes, but he's too weak.

I'm afraid that I am imposing life on him, that my decisions have doomed him to an existence of misery and pain. I am deciding not only his fate, but our entire family's. If we go through with this tracheostomy, he may remain a helpless, crazy man in a bed for the rest of his life. Or, even if his mind does return to normal, he still may remain ventilator-dependent and confined to a bed forever, and Ray and I will have to find a way to take care of both him and our mother. Or, in the best-case scenario, if his mind returns to normal and he tries to wean off of the ventilator and physically rehabilitate, he will face the greatest, most daunting fight of his life. But if we don't go through with this tracheostomy then I will lose my father, probably today.

Lenea, one of the PAs, enters the room. Her demeanor seems intentionally casual, as if she sees us about to jump off a building and she's here to talk us down off the ledge. She runs through the pros and cons of the different options again, and then she says, "What I see is a room full of people who love the man in this bed and aren't ready to let him go yet," which makes me start to cry. I nod in agreement. I am not ready to let him go. My mother cries and nods, too.

We agree to intubation again, with the understanding that they will perform the tracheostomy as soon as possible. We leave the room so that Lenea and the respiratory therapists can intubate him.

I storm out of the ICU and run down the hallway with the ugly blue and gray carpet, past the elevators and the information desk, and through the front doors of the hospital. I find myself caught in the rage of a summer thunderstorm as I run to my parents' old, beige minivan. When I get to the car, I slam the driver's side door shut so hard that it breaks and I can't get the door to latch completely. I cry and scream, bang my hands and head against the steering wheel, slam the door repeatedly against the frame of the car. My cell phone rings; it's my mother. "Where did you go? You have to come back! I need you! He's trying to throw up the tube! He's fighting against the restraints! He's so miserable! What have we done? Did we make a mistake? Where the hell did you go?! Come back. I NEED YOU!"

# Impending Eviction

NORTH CAROLINA, JUNE 2010

PROGRESS NOTES:          06/17/10          10:05

61 yo male with long hospital course. Re admitted to ICU secondary to massive GI bleed from gastric remnant. S/p resection of bleeding remnant, repair of G-J leak, and J tube placement on 6/3. . .

Respiratory failure: S/p trach 6/16. Lighten sedation, progress to trach collar trials today.

GI bleed: Continues to have high output from his L abdominal JP drain which is placed near the G-J anastamosis [sic] where a small leak is still present. . .


PROGRESS NOTES:          06/19/10          08:49

More alert this am, still on pressure support MV, did not do trach collar trial 6/18 as still somnolent. . .

Very alert this am, attempted trach collar trial but pt lasted < 1 minute due to increased work of breathing and dropping O2 stats. . .

Dispo: pt accepted to select, likely transfer on Monday 6/21.


AFTER INTUBATING MY father on Saturday, June 12, we were told that the earliest the general surgeon could perform the tracheostomy was the afternoon of Wednesday, June 16, so he ended up spending four days tied to the bed with a tube down his throat. It was during this time that I was informed that my father would have to leave the ICU again. Even though he was still in critical condition and still had a leak, they wanted to kick him out. (And the "they" was always ambiguous—news of this sort was almost always communicated to me by a social worker, who usually claimed that "they" was the insurance company. However, given the way that the rest of the summer played out, I think that the surgeons, ICU doctors, and/or social workers may have had more power over the situation than they liked to admit, so perhaps they were also part of the "they"?)

My father would have to move to a long-term care facility that had the ability to care for ventilator-dependent patients. I was told that there were only six such facilities in the entire state of North Carolina, and only four of those were within a reasonable driving distance: one in Raleigh, two in Greensboro, and one on the seventh floor of the very same hospital in which my father currently resided, which was called Select. I made appointments to visit all four.

Of the many possible fates worse than death, living in one of these facilities must rank high on the list. They are the places where the elderly and infirm (most of whom have been mostly forgotten by the rest of the world) are sent to die. These individuals lie in beds beside noisy, hot machines that breathe for them as they are tended to by under-paid, overworked staff whose main goal is to keep the patients alive yet docile, sus-pended in a medical purgatory. At the end of each of my visits, I felt like I couldn't walk to my car fast enough—like sticky tentacles might reach through the front doors of the building and drag me back in.

The one in Raleigh was too far and too hot; the air-conditioning in the building was broken, and industrial-sized fans placed in the halls just circulated the rank, humid air. One of the facilities in Greensboro constituted an entire floor of an enormous hospital, and I determined that my mother's mobility issues would make it practically impossi-ble for her to visit. The other place in Greensboro was dirty and depressing. The best choice was Select, the facility located inside the hospital we were already in. I met with the director, toured the premises, and told him that we were very interested in moving my father there. Some of the nurses in the ICU told me that they had heard "horror stories" about some of the things that had happened there, but they agreed with me that it was the best option. Especially, they said, because they knew that I would continue to be present and vigilant.

Select's greatest strength was its location; if my father had another medical emergency and required the care of Dr. Belfore, then he could be transferred back to the ICU immediately. A representative from Select visited the ICU to examine my father and look at his chart, and shortly thereafter we were accepted.

On the morning of the day we were supposed to transfer, bright red blood started seeping out of one of my father's abdominal drains around 9:15. About two hours later, I found myself sitting next to my father's gurney in the radiology department as we waited for an emergency CT scan. The next day he vomited blood and his blood pressure plummeted. I remember feeling at that point like we were trapped inside some sort of dark comedy where every step forward must necessarily be squashed by unexpected, impeccably timed hardships.

A few days later, we were informed that Select would no longer accept my father as a patient. He was "too much of a risk."

# You Are Jim Blevins. You Are in the HOSPITAL. It Is ~~May~~ June.

NORTH CAROLINA, JUNE 2010

EXACTLY FIVE DAYS after the tracheostomy, I noticed a change in my father as soon as I walked in his room that morning. When he saw me, he started gesturing with his hands in an attempt to communicate something. He couldn't speak because of the trach, so I handed him a pen and a pad of paper. He wrote, "Newspaper?" Surprised by his sudden sanity, I asked, "Do you want a newspaper, Daddy?" He nodded and made a circular gesture with his hand. "You want me to bring you a newspaper every day?" I asked. He nodded again.

My stomach lurched excitedly, and I teared up a little. Before the gastric bypass, my father had always started his mornings by reading the newspaper and drinking a cup of coffee. That morning, June 21, was the first time since late March that he had asked for a newspaper. So with one messily scrawled word and a question mark, I had my proof that Jim Blevins was back.

We spent the rest of the day trying to communicate. He didn't have the strength and dexterity necessary to write legibly with the pen and paper, so his side of the conversation was very limited. He wanted to know what had happened; he couldn't remember anything since the morning of the first surgery. "That's probably a very good thing, Daddy," I said. "I don't think you'd want to remember it." He listened with wide eyes as I relayed a bullet point version of the previous three months. I told him how resilient he had been, how close he'd come to death. He was The Boy Who Lived, I said. A total badass. He kept mouthing the word "wow" and shaking his head, clearly thrilled and relieved to be alive, and it seemed like he was getting his second wind. I told him that the biggest hurdles ahead (other than fixing the leak) were weaning him off the ventilator and restoring his physical strength, and that getting him well and out of that bed was presently my full-time job. He seemed excited. As I had suspected, he liked knowing that he was a badass underdog—King Henry on Saint Crispin's Day and all that.

As soon as I left the hospital that day, I went to Office Depot and bought a small dry-erase board and a pack of markers. The board would become our primary mode of communication for the rest of the summer. I also bought a variety of posters and stickers. I created two motivational posters, one for vent weaning and another for physical therapy, and hung them on the wall across from the foot of his bed. For every hour he spent off the vent, he got a monkey sticker (a banana sticker for every half hour). After every PT session, I would ask the physical therapists to put stars on the PT poster for that day. I wanted him to be able to track his progress and see a visual representation of how far he'd come. I transcribed the poem "Invictus" onto poster board and hung it beside the bed. One of the nurses resurrected the "You are Jim Blevins. You are in the HOSPITAL. It is May" poster, placed a piece of medical tape over the word "May," and wrote "June." We hung up all of the cards that people had sent my father over the previous three months. It was perhaps the craftiest and most like a first-grade teacher I've ever been in my life. I was determined as hell to get him out of that bed. I was going to save him.

Years later, I'm still not sure whether 2010 taught me that you can't save the people you love, or that you can. I know that my daily vigilance and advocacy on my father's behalf significantly improved his odds of survival. Because I helped and supported her (but tried not to wait on her), my mother grew stronger and more independent. But that strength didn't last very long, and I imagine that her version of the story would be that she became more independent in spite of me, not because of me. And in the weeks and months that followed the tracheostomy, my father descended into the deepest depression I've ever witnessed. Apparently cute monkey and banana stickers were not enough to instill him with the will to live. As my friend Stacy had predicted, I watched him give up. I gave up, too, at times.

Once the imminent threat of death was behind us, my overextended endorphins deflated. For months I had been living in crisis mode, intentionally remaining focused on the day-to-day dramas and not the larger picture. But when the goal shifted from survival to rehabilitation, I started thinking about me again.

My body had changed. The muscle definition I had gained from my years of intense workouts in New York was gone. My shoulders sagged. My skin had become sallow and lined. I had put on weight and gotten a series of embarrassing haircuts from subpar local hairdressers. I developed a hard, round lump on my neck that gradually grew bigger and I eventually had to have surgically removed.

For months my primary emotions had been anger and terror, and I continually bounced between the two in a seemingly never-ending loop. Once I allowed myself the indulgence of thinking about *my* future, I became hopeless and depressed. I was so entrenched in my parents' care that I couldn't see a way out. I had no employment prospects and was dependent on my parents for money. I was in the midst of a divorce, sending legal documents back and forth to New York via FedEx. At times I thought that maybe my mother was right—maybe Jennifer's life *was* ruined.

But then there was Gail. Funny, levelheaded Gail.

One day the two of us were sitting in the ICU waiting room, waiting for the call to let us know that we could go back and see my father. I was in a particularly catastrophic mood that day and started venting to Gail, listing out all of the bleak future scenarios that I had been envisioning for my family and me, and all of the potential impediments I foresaw. Gail stopped me and said, "You know what your problem is? You think too much. You and your whole family—y'all just think too much. Always thinking. You go outside and see that the sky is blue and need to know all the reasons why it's blue, and worry if it'll still be blue tomorrow. I go outside, see that the sky is blue, and think, 'Great—it's blue again today!' and go about my business. You just need to stop *thinking* so much."

Gail regularly reminded me that I had had my own life before my father's gastric bypass surgery and reassured me that I would have my own life again one day. She emphasized that focusing on my own future was not selfish but necessary, and that I must move ahead with that future as soon as possible.

If anybody did any saving that year, I think it was Gail saving me. Or, perhaps more accurately, Gail helped me save myself. Which, I suppose, is what I did for my father. And which, I suppose, is the most that any of us can ever do for the people we love.

# PT and TCTs

## NORTH CAROLINA, JULY 2010

PROGRESS NOTES:          07/05/2010

Neuro: Alert, distress. Valium prn anxiety [for] TCT.

GI: Not stable, [no] further GI bleeding.


EXAMINATION: 7103 - CXR PORTABLE EXAM      Jul 5 2010

REASON: RESPIRATORY DISTRESS

FINDINGS: Tracheostomy tube, right-sided PICC line and EKG leads redemonstrated. Hazy densities over the lower two-thirds of the hemithorax on each side consistent with underlying effusion. Coexisting pneumonia/atelectasis cannot be excluded. Overall no change.


HE QUICKLY ADAPTS to writing on the dry-erase board. One of the first things he writes is, "When I can eat and drink again, what can I dream about eating and drinking?"

After the initial excitement about the news of his survival has passed, the depression starts to set in quickly. Once he begins physical therapy and discovers how weak and debilitated he is, he begins to understand how much excruciating work lies ahead of him. When he starts his trach collar trials (or, TCTs) to wean off of the ventilator, he discovers how frail his lungs have become. There is no quick fix for coming back from the dead.

I coordinate with the ICU team and his physical therapists to try to maximize each day. I arrive by nine every morning, and the physical therapists arrive shortly thereafter. We quickly discover that his PT sessions are much more successful when he remains on the ventilator for them. Also, he works harder at PT if I'm there to push him. When he communicates to the therapists that he wants to stop, they have to stop; when he signals to me that he wants to stop, I'm usually able to encourage him to work a little while longer. He doesn't like disappointing me.

After PT, we begin the TCT. A respiratory therapist disconnects the ventilator tube from the collar around my father's neck and puts a tiny oxygen mask over the cylinder protruding from the hole in his throat. During one of his visits, Ray hooks a DVD player up to the TV in the room so that we can watch movies together while he's vent weaning. Sometimes I purposely bring in movies that depict bleaker situations than our own to give us a sense of perspective. When we watch *War of the Worlds*, I pause after father-and-daughter team Tom Cruise and Dakota Fanning get sucked up into the belly of a Tripod to await certain death and say, "Look, Daddy—things could be worse. Aliens could be using us as fertilizer."

We watch CNN together, and I fill him in on the oil spill in the Gulf. "There's an oil well leaking into the Gulf, just like you've been leaking," I tell him. We watch footage of shiny black creatures crawling on beaches, and well-paid white men deflecting blame. I'm beginning to feel like both disasters will go on forever.

He develops significant anxiety around the trach collar trials. On his dry-erase board, he explains to me that being off the vent feels like he's drowning, or dying. The doctors prescribe Valium to calm him down during the TCTs, but it doesn't really help. Often-times if I leave the ICU to pee during a TCT, he'll page a nurse and get them to put him back on the ventilator before I've returned. He's supposed to increase by an hour every day, but he has actually been decreasing his time off the vent recently.

If my mother is the one with him during a TCT, she will immediately page a nurse to put him back on the vent as soon as he expresses anxiety or discomfort. She can't stand to see him in pain. It frustrates me, because I know that our only hope of getting him out of that bed is getting him off of that machine. Our different approaches to my father's vent weaning have been reminding me of my first (and only) day of soccer practice.

We moved from Winston-Salem to Charlotte the summer before I started second grade, and my parents enrolled my brother and me in soccer lessons shortly after we got there. I had never played soccer in my life, and I had no idea what the rules were or what the hell you were supposed to do. Ray and I were in different age groups, so on the first day of practice I walked into a group of complete strangers, most of whom already knew each other. As I fumbled around and made countless mistakes, I could hear some of the other kids laughing at me and talking about me behind my back. When the practice ended, I ran crying in the direction of my parents. I encountered my father first, who kneeled down and asked me why I was crying. When I told him how horrible it had been and that I never wanted to go back, he said, "But you have to go back! You can't quit something just because it's hard." I broke away from him and ran to my mother, who was standing by the car. I repeated my lament, and she said, "Oh honey, you don't ever have to go back to that horrible place and those nasty people!" And I never did.

I have always viewed that experience as a defining moment of my childhood. It was one of the last times I sided with my mother and took the easy way out. As I grew older, I gradually started actively seeking out challenges that scared me and made me uncomfortable. I decided early on that I wanted to be more like my father—levelheaded, ambitious, dependable, and restrained—than my mother, who I saw as volatile, unpredictable, unreliable, and overly passionate.

I feel like the only way my father is going to rehabilitate is if I can get him to follow the same advice he gave me on the soccer field that day. Recently he's been acting more and more like my mother, though, which scares the hell out of me.

# Legacy, Part II

NOWHERE AND EVERYWHERE, THE PRESENT

ONE AFTERNOON DURING the early days of our disaster, I was in the ICU waiting room with my mother and someone else (I can't recall who). My mother, who was sitting across from me, suddenly exclaimed, "Wow! You have such beautiful eyes!" She sounded like she was surprised—like it was the first time she had ever noticed that I have beautiful eyes. The other person and I exchanged a look of disbelief. My eyes are my defining feature; they're usually the first characteristic that people notice and comment on when they meet me. At the time, I was a little pissed. Did it really take my mother thirty-one years to notice that I have beautiful eyes?

After years of reflecting on this moment (and countless other moments), and after years of trying to find a way to portray my mother accurately and fairly in my writing, I have concluded that yes, it probably did take my mother thirty-one years to notice the fact that I have beautiful eyes. My mother could not see me. Gail even confirmed as much one night when we were sitting in her living room watching TV. When I said that I felt like my mother didn't see who I really was, Gail teared up as she said, "Yes, and it makes me sad for her, because she'll probably never know you, and you're a really fantastic person."

But I have come to realize that what I interpreted as blindness or disdain at the time was actually a much more complicated dynamic that existed between us. All of the times she bemoaned my "terrible skin," all of the times she told me that I needed to lose weight or look like someone else, every time she fixated on some perceived flaw or failing, the criticisms she was hurling at me were actually directed at herself. It was more than a simple case of projecting her insecurities onto me; I believe that she really had trouble seeing me as a separate being from her. So, in other words, commenting on my terrible skin was an act of self-loathing. Telling me I was too fat was self-criticism. I was supposed to be a better version of her—the one who had the brother and father she didn't, the one who got to live the life full of achievements and thinness that she had not. She criticized me when I was not the ideal her, yet she was jealous of me when I was.

I feel like I have no choice but to conclude that if my mother was not able to see me, then I have never been able to truly see her.

I don't believe that this is true of all mother/daughter relationships. I know of mothers and daughters who have healthy relationships, in which they're allowed to exist and flourish as separate individuals. But in my matrilineage, the act of individuation was seen as a betrayal. A crime. I believe that the only people who can truly understand this dynamic are mothers and daughters who have experienced it firsthand. My father has certainly never understood it. He would get so exasperated when Granny, my mother, and I would fight, and he would just chalk it up to some generic belief about mothers and daughters never getting along.

I don't know how to describe to you the love that existed between the three of us because I was in it, and I'm still in it. It is not a safe love. Even though both Granny and my mother are now dead, I still spend my days navigating that dangerous and obsessive love. I am trying to prove to them that I can not be them and still love them.

And I do love them. Fiercely.

# Stent #2, Surgery #7

NORTH CAROLINA, JULY 2010

DATE OF SURGERY: 07/07/2010

PREOPERATIVE DIAGNOSIS: Status post Roux-en-Y gastric bypass with anastomotic leak and status post gastrectomy of the remnant stomach.

PROCEDURE: Esophagogastroduodenoscopy with upper GI stent placement.

HE OPENS HIS mouth and screams but produces no sound. I stand in a corner of the room and watch my father's face contort in agony as a team of six people transfers him from his hospital bed to a gurney. Once he's secured on the gurney, they disconnect him from the ventilator. The respiratory therapist immediately places a bag-valve mask over the tube protruding from his neck and begins to manually administer oxygen. The nurse hooks him up to the small monitor hanging off the edge of the gurney so she can continue to track his heart rate, blood pressure, and oxygen levels as they travel to surgery. She places his chart, which now fills two large blue binders, on the gurney between his feet. Swaddled in blankets and too weak to move, my father resembles a baby. A 350-pound, battered baby. He looks around the room and tries to locate me. His eyes are panicked, hungry, and wide.

"I'm right here, Daddy," I tell him from the corner.

When his eyes find me, he nods. It's a nod of acknowledgment but also agreement, as if he's agreeing with me that I am right here. As if right here is the only place I could possibly be. Because if I were not here, he would be dead. So because he is alive, I am here.

Yes, I am here. I am so fucking here that I have become part of this room, part of this transformation. I could not possibly be more fucking *here*.

Dr. Belfore is trying another stent procedure to fix the leak. Today she's putting in two stents instead of one in the hopes that they won't migrate this time. Given the fact that the last stent procedure didn't work, my expectations for this one are very low. But, fortunately this situation has helped keep us in the ICU longer. Since Select rejected my father in late June, the social worker assigned to his case has been trying to find another placement. So far, no one wants to take him because of his continued GI problems. They can't transfer us back to the bariatric wing on the sixth floor because the ICU is the only department in the hospital (other than Select) with the capability of treating ventilator-dependent patients. As far as I'm concerned, the longer we stay in the ICU the better. The staff in here is excellent, and they know us well. Also, they've basically become my social circle. I find it hard to remember a time when my life extended beyond the walls of this hospital.

After my father is wheeled away to his seventh surgery, I sit in the green vinyl recliner next to the bed and turn on the TV. By habit, I automatically turn to CNN to check on the oil spill, now in its seventy-ninth day. Sanjay Gupta's head hovers next to live footage from the underwater spill cam. He interviews a doctor from BP about the potential health consequences for the cleanup workers in the Gulf. The BP doctor's answers are as slippery as the oil spreading across the surface of the water. Seventy-nine days into the disaster and they still don't know how to fix the leak. Gupta asks some guy standing in front of a big computer screen displaying fancy graphics what will happen if BP is never able to stop the spill. The guy assures us not to worry about such a scenario, but then concedes that the leak could spill oil into the Gulf for years if someone doesn't figure out how to stop it.

One hundred and six days into my father's disaster and the days now ooze into each other. I pull my peanut butter and banana sandwich out of its Ziploc bag and sink my teeth into the gooey, fruity nuttiness. I do not believe that today's surgery will fix my father's leak. He will keep leaking, the oil in the Gulf will keep leaking, and I will be here. Always here, always watching.

# I See Fat People

THE MOMENT I encounter a fat person out in the world, I am internally assailed by contradictory impulses. The first, most instinctual response is revulsion. Decades of conditioning have hardwired me to perceive fat as a moral failing and disease—contradictory beliefs that most of us don't question. But since my father's experience has caused me to question these contradictions, the revulsion I feel when I see a fat person is now quickly replaced by sympathy. In the random fat person attempting to inconspicuously live their life in a public space, I see my parents. I see a potential future self. I see someone living in a world that wasn't built for them—a world that, in fact, actively seeks to annihilate them.

But pity is offensive, patronizing. So my sympathy eventually morphs into anger and frustration. I get angry at myself for pitying the fat person, and I get angry at our fat-hating society for marginalizing the fat person. I feel frustrated because I don't know how to feel about the fat person. They don't want my pity. They don't want me to openly celebrate the fact that they have the courage to be fat out in the world. I imagine that, more than anything, they just don't want me to see them as a *fat person*. They simply want to be seen as a *person*, out and about in a public space, living their life.

I think about this issue a lot when I read through my father's medical records from 2010, because I can see how my father was perceived by the medical personnel that tended to him. After poring through almost 1,500 pages of records written by a variety of authors, I have discerned concerning patterns. His fat, his "morbid obesity," is a reoccurring fixation, even in instances when it seems totally irrelevant to the matter at hand. Oftentimes his "large body habitus" is cited as an impediment, a reason why a test may not be accurate, or why a procedure may not yield positive results. It is as if his fat body presents itself as a blanket excuse for any failure on their part, and as if it relegates him to second-class citizenship.

Studies have shown that many medical practitioners are biased against fat patients. More than half of the 620 primary care physicians in one study "viewed obese patients as awkward, unattractive, ugly, and noncompliant." Another study of almost 5,000 first-year medical students found that "a majority of students exhibited implicit (74%) and

136

explicit (67%) weight bias," and that their explicit attitudes were "more negative toward obese people than toward racial minorities, gays, lesbians, and poor people." Even health professionals who specialize in treating obesity exhibit implicit and explicit bias against fat patients; in 2003, researchers determined that the "obesity specialists" in their study "associated the stereotypes lazy, stupid, and worthless with obese people," even though the group was comprised of medical practitioners who understood that "obesity is caused by genetic and environmental factors and is not simply a function of individual behavior."

This widespread bias against fat patients causes many to avoid seeking medical care, sometimes for very serious issues, because they're tired of being told that all of their problems (from an ear infection to chest pain) are caused by their fat. When they do seek care, serious conditions are sometimes misdiagnosed because their physicians attribute their symptoms to their weight. In only seeing body size, such physicians fail to really see a patient's body.

When I read through the language used in my father's medical records, I can tell that the authors see his body, but they also don't see it. His fat body is often depicted as a barrier or obstacle to overcome. Many of the health professionals who chronicled my father's story seem oblivious to the power of language, to the detrimental effect that word choice can have on real lives. Even when they appear to compliment him they do him a disservice; the repeated insistence on how "pleasant" the "obese white male" in the bed is paints my father as a sort of Santa Claus—jolly and likable, in spite of his fat. Also, the emphasis on his "whiteness" in the medical records makes me wonder how differently he might have been perceived (and treated) if he had been a person of color, instead of a "pleasant" old white man.

I have to believe that if the medical community (and the rest of the world) truly *saw* fat bodies, then more would be done to provide appropriate medical equipment and devise more reliable tests and procedures for fat patients. They wouldn't cite fat bodies as excuses for the limitations of their practices and procedures. They might be more hesitant to irrevocably alter perfectly functioning digestive systems in the name of "health."

In *The Hyper(in)visible Fat Woman: Weight and Gender Discourse in Contemporary Society*, Jeannine A. Gailey writes, "Fat presents an *apparent* paradox because it is visible and dissected publicly; in this respect, it is *hypervisible*. Fat is also marginalized and erased; in this respect, it is *hyperinvisible*." Fat people are invisible, yet simultaneously overly visible. We don't really see them, yet we can't *not* see them. They're like ubiquitous ninjas, or like those 3-D posters that used to be for sale in mall kiosks—the ones where you have to tilt your head and look at the image just so in order to see the 3-D dolphin or whatnot hidden within the bigger picture. At the height of their popularity in the 1990s, those posters were all over the place. Everyone saw them, but not everyone could see beyond the surface image.

I've never been able to see the hidden image in any of those 3-D posters. Not a single one. But I see fat people all the time. And maybe one day I'll be able to see them without projecting my long, complicated personal history with fat onto them. Maybe one day when I encounter fat people out in the world, I will be able to see their stories instead of my own.

# The Decubitus

NORTH CAROLINA, JULY 2010

EXAMINATION: 7355 - UGI W/KUB      Jul 8 2010

REASON: CHECK FOR LEAK

FINDINGS: After swallowing Gastrografin and barium, there is filling of the a [sic] small gastric pouch and the proximal aspect of the stent. Contrast is seen to swirl within the stent, suggesting that there is standing fluid in the stent rather than a definite stricture. Obstruction or stricture beyond this point cannot be excluded, however, particularly since the contrast is never seen to go beyond the distal aspect of the stent. There is no definite evidence of anastomotic leak.

THE DAY AFTER the second stent procedure, my father and I made another trip down to radiology for yet another swallow study. For the first time, we received good news: There was no evidence of a leak. The stents seemed to be doing their job. On July 15, exactly one week later, a new capping system on the Macondo well stopped the flow of oil in the Gulf for the first time since the Deepwater Horizon explosion in April. Neither leak was completely resolved yet, but things were looking up.

Dr. Belfore planned to keep the stents in until the first week of August, so our residence in the ICU was secure until that point. The time between the two procedures was to be devoted to progressing with both PT and vent weaning. Also, he could begin having small sips of clear liquids now that there was proof that the stents were working.

Those weeks between the stent placement and their removal were some of the darkest, most hopeless weeks for my father. His anxiety about the trach collar trials and physical therapy increased, and his depression deepened. The sips of clear liquids usually just made him throw up, so getting to drink again wasn't even that rewarding. Also, a bedsore was discovered near his sacrum, and it grew rapidly. The first mention of the wound that I can find in the medical records is on July 17 ("Decubitus Ulcer: L buttock, causing pain for pt when sitting in chair, continue wound care"), but I know that it was bothering him earlier than that. The decubitus eventually burrowed all the way to his sacrum—all the way to the bone. It caused my father considerable pain during physical therapy, and it made him even more anxious. He knew that bed sores could be fatal; they had contributed to his own mother's death a few years earlier.

The fact that my father received little to no nutrition for most of the month of April was a big part of the reason why he suddenly found himself with a big hole in his lower back. His body was simply ravaged. He was so weak, so debilitated that he started to give up. One of the ICU doctors had a long talk with him one day, trying to get to the bottom of his anxiety about the vent weaning. The doctor asked him if he believed that he would one day get off of the ventilator and out of a hospital bed. My father shook his head no.

I ran out of ways to encourage him. Nothing I was doing seemed to be helping. Mentally and emotionally, he seemed to be so far away from me. I thought that after everything he'd been through that I was going to lose him after all.

It was difficult to know where to direct my anger (which was, at times, almost paralyzing). We have never been able to definitively prove why my father's gastric bypass surgery went so very wrong, so while it was convenient to direct my anger at Dr. Belfore, I was never really sure if she deserved it. Some days I was angry at my parents for getting so fat, but even at the time I was able to see that the issue was far more complex than that. Fat was an easy culprit. Maybe that's part of the reason why it is framed as the culprit so frequently in our culture.

When I turned on the TV and saw images of the ongoing devastation in the Gulf of Mexico, I had a clear place to direct my anger about the oil spill: BP. The TV told me that the disaster had been caused by the company's negligence; therefore, BP was responsible. But then years later when I began to research the oil spill, I discovered that even though BP *was* at fault, the general corruption of the oil industry (which, in some ways, extended to the US Government) made placing blame a bit trickier.

I've always found it interesting that in so many books, articles, and television shows about the "obesity epidemic," people are constantly seeking someone or something to blame, as if identifying the root of the problem is possible. As if there *is* one root, or only a few. As if directing our collective anger about fat at any particular source could somehow help quell the anger, or erase the fat.

# Full Disclosure

I FEEL THE need to clarify something.

I know that just as I entered my father's gastric bypass experience with deeply entrenched feelings about fat, you opened this book having your own deeply entrenched opinions on the subject. By this point, I imagine that you've read things that have either challenged or confirmed what you believe. You may think that my father's case represents an anomalous instance of modern medicine gone wrong, and that gastric bypass is still the best/only way to combat the disease of obesity; you might think that gastric bypass involves mutilating a healthy digestive system and is just another way to oppress (or sometimes kill) fat people. You may think that diets and weight loss products are still the ideal method for losing weight, and that people like my parents are just too weak, lazy, or damaged to succeed on a diet; you might be convinced that diets are ineffective time and money wasters, and that losing weight and keeping it off long-term is not possible. You may believe that fat is the primary cause of a multitude of health problems, and that anyone who suggests otherwise is "glorifying obesity"; you might think that fat itself is not an indicator of health. You may believe any of these things. To be completely honest with you, I'm still not entirely sure what *I* believe.

When J. Eric Oliver, a former Robert Wood Johnson Health Policy Research Scholar at Yale University and professor of Political Science at the University of Chicago, set out to write the book that would become *Fat Politics: The Real Story behind America's Obesity Epidemic*, he initially thought he was going to write a book about "why we were gaining so much weight and what we could do to stop it." However, after delving into the research, he changed his course. He discovered that many of the facts and findings that have been presented by the medical industry are based on "very shaky evidence" and "weak…statistical claims," and to him what was "an epidemic began to look a lot more like a politically orchestrated campaign to capitalize on America's growing weight." For instance, he learned that the two studies (both published in the *Journal of the American Medical Association*) which proclaimed that obesity was killing hundreds of thousands of Americans a year—studies that effectively kicked off the US "War on Obesity"— employed questionable methodology, such as attributing the deaths of *all* obese people to their fat, even if they had died from a snakebite or a car crash. He also learned that the BMI chart was created by a Belgian astronomer in the 1830s—not a doctor practicing modern-day medicine—yet is currently touted by the American Medical Association as the primary tool for diagnosing obesity.

I won't go into detail about his many other important findings, because you can read his book if you're interested in them. You could also read Glenn A. Gaesser's *Big Fat Lies*, Paul Campos's *The Obesity Myth*, Linda Bacon's *Health at Every Size*, Harriet Brown's *Body of Truth*, and many other books and studies that have come to similar conclusions.

It is absolutely possible that some of these authors have committed transgressions similar to those committed by some of the authors, doctors, and researchers firmly situated on the other side of the debate. It's possible that they skewed findings or misrepresented statistics to further their own agenda. I'm not saying that I think they did—I'm simply acknowledging a potential counterargument.

I should also disclose that prior to delving into my research about the "obesity epidemic" following my father's surgery, I knew nothing about the history of fat activists who have been fighting against weight-based oppression since the late 1960s. Sondra Solovay's *Tipping the Scales of Justice* and Marilyn Wann's *FAT!SO?* were the first books I came across that introduced me to the world of fat activism. Recently published books such as *The Body is Not an Apology* by Sonya Renee Taylor and *You Have the Right to Remain Fat* by Virgie Tovar build on the work of activists like Solovay and Wann, and Charlotte Cooper's *Fat Activism* offers a compelling history and analysis of the movement.

Also compelling are historical accounts of the evolution of dieting and cultural perceptions of fat, such as Hillel Schwartz's *Never Satisfied*, Peter N. Stearns's *Fat History*, and Amy Erdman Farrell's *Fat Shame*. It might be harder to immediately dismiss the claims made in books like *Fat Politics* and *The Obesity Myth* after learning that "[c]oncern about weight and dieting is not timeless; its origins are modern and can be quite precisely traced," origins which Stearns traces to the 1890s in America (slightly earlier in England). He observes that public condemnation of fat and prejudice against fat bodies in the fashion industry preceded concern about fat within the medical community. At the turn of the century, "much of the causation of the growing medical concern about weight came from patient pressure, rather than the other way around." In other words, society decided that fat was bad years before doctors did. For me, knowing more about fat's fluctuant history has made it harder to blindly accept modern-day anti-fat discourse. This is not to say that I don't believe any of it—just that I now better understand what Schwartz means when he argues, "Weight is a cultural condition."

Even so, I still have very mixed feelings about fat. I have seen with my own eyes how fat can adversely affect a person's life. I continue to obsess about my own weight, even after everything I've read and experienced since 2010, and I feel like a hypocrite for it. I am still a little fucked up about fat. In many ways I'm still that six-year-old girl in the backseat of my mother's car, asking permission to detach my head and put it on a skinnier body. I don't have any answers for you. All I know is that fat is an incredibly complex subject—way more complex than we've been led to believe, and that vilifying fat people is myopic, ignorant, and cruel.

I learned in Stearns's book that the word "diet" didn't obtain its modern meaning until 1910, which is also the year that Granny was born. My grandmother, mother, and I represent three generations of women in the US who were born and raised in a society that aggressively conditions women to remain perpetually dissatisfied with their bodies. I know that, realistically, I can't expect to expel the century of anti-fat messages that have leaked into my psyche within a few years, or maybe even in my lifetime. But I can remain aware and continue to question anything that is presented to me as definitive "truth" about fat.

So I suppose what I want to clarify is this: I am still skeptical. I think that you should be, too.

# Frodo and Sam

NORTH CAROLINA, JULY 2010

*7/30/2010: He is changing right in front of me. He is not the same father anymore. He looks to me to fix it. They all look to me. I hate them for it.*

THE FIRST THING he did every morning when I walked in his room was hand me the dry-erase board, which was usually covered with instructions and complaints. Items he wanted me to bring him. Requests he wanted me to make on his behalf. Queries about his instructions from the day before. It was the same with my mother—every exchange consisted of a list of all of the things that I must do for her, and all of the things that I did for her that I had done incorrectly.

My resentment grew. I had not walked away from my life in New York to watch him surrender or to become their handmaid. I had never seriously entertained the possibility that he would give up if he were given the chance to heal. This was not the Jim Blevins that I had known for thirty-one years. I didn't know what else I could say or do to get him to fight.

One day he had a particularly terrible physical therapy session. He had made progress the day before, almost standing up for the first time in four months *while* off the ventilator. But the next day he couldn't even manage to sit up on the side of the bed for more than a few seconds. He became anxious and scared, and signaled wildly to be put back on the ventilator. The physical therapists had to give up only a few minutes into the session and page the nurse to get him settled back in bed.

After he was back on the vent and under the covers, the nurse dimmed the lights and everyone left the room. My father started crying—a completely noiseless cry because of the trach. I held his hand and said, "It's OK, Daddy. You'll do better tomorrow." He started shaking his head, and the silent crying intensified. I realized that he was saying something. At first I couldn't tell what it was, but then I managed to read his lips. He was saying the words, "I'm a failure, I'm a failure," over and over again. He wouldn't even look at me; he kept shaking his head with his eyes closed, repeating those voiceless words.

In that moment, I suddenly got it. My overachieving, my self-loathing, my drive to single-handedly "save" my father—it all made sense. In that excruciatingly sad moment, watching my frail, depressed, demoralized father silently beat himself up for being a failure, I saw myself. Against epic hardships, experiencing blinding pain, my father could only see that he was not enough, could only see his weakness. And I could see that by modeling myself after my father, I had adopted his insistence on unconquerable perfection, his belief that we are the masters of our fates, the captains of our souls.

Except, of course, we really aren't. We are delicate bodies with assailable souls. We are just two mortal humans, trying to do the best we can for the people we love. And one day, he *will* die. I won't be able to save him from the monsters in the front yard, or the diamond mine in the basement. I will bury him in the cemetery plot next to all of the people who were in that dream, and, when I do, it won't mean that either one of us was a failure.

As he cried, I held his hand and reminded him of how far he had come. I pointed to the dozens of monkey and banana stickers on his vent weaning poster, the stars on his PT poster. I told him again how close he had come to death, how brave he had been, and I stressed that giving up today didn't mean that he was giving up forever. "We do have to get the ring to Mordor, Daddy," I said. "But we don't have to get there today."

# Legacy, Part III, or Try Not to Get Any Fatter

NEW YORK, MAY 2014

My FATHER TEETERS across the uneven ground, using his cane to balance as we weave through hundred-year-old gravestones and search for the one whose story we've heard a hundred times. The sky is a brilliant blue, and the sun shines brightly between small, puffy, slow-moving clouds. It's a cool, breezy May afternoon in Queens, and we've come to Calvary Cemetery to bring my mother home.

Walking with us across the shaggy, overgrown grass are three of my mother's first cousins—Stephen, Kenneth, and Linda, and her best friend since college, Diana. Deborah, Diana's daughter, walks by her mother's side. Only a few years apart in age, Deborah and I haven't seen each other since we were kids. I don't know when any of these people who love my mother last saw her, but I'm pretty sure it's been at least ten to twenty years.

Also in attendance is Jack, who brought his camera and has offered to document the event. Jack and his girlfriend Mariah are hosting the two of us in their Brooklyn apartment this weekend, where my father is sleeping in the guest room. I'm on the couch.

My mother has been dead for four months, and her absence has created a deafening void. In the end, her end came so quickly that, months later, it still seems surreal. Distracted by finishing a graduate degree in North Carolina and then moving to South Carolina to pursue two more, I didn't realize how rapidly my mother had been declining in the six months before her death, in part because my father concealed the severity of her condition from Ray and me until she had to be hospitalized. She died on January 29, 2014. The death certificate lists the cause of death as congestive heart failure. Granny's cause of death was also congestive heart failure. Frederick, my maternal grandfather, died of a heart attack at the age of forty-two. I will endeavor to take care of my heart.

Today my heart pumps blood, my lungs breathe air, and I carry my mother's ashes in my purse. When my brother, father, and I sat in a room at hospice with a man from the crematorium (the same man who charged us an extra $300 because of my mother's body weight) a mere hour after she stopped breathing, Ray was the only one of us with the presence of mind to think about Calvary. We had planned on burying all of her ashes in our family plot in a cemetery in the mountains of North Carolina (where my father is from), but when the crematorium man asked if we would like him to retain some of the ashes to spread elsewhere, Ray pointed out that she would have liked to have some taken to Calvary. So that's why I now have a small cardboard box with my mother's name printed on top sitting in the top of my purse. Ray recently started a new job and couldn't get off work, so my father and I have had to make this pilgrimage without him.

As we near the grave, Stephen takes the lead. In the early 1990s, he and my mother spent years researching their shared genealogy, which runs on my maternal grandfather's branch of the family tree. In those pre-internet, pre-Ancestry.com days, Stephen and my mother corresponded with municipal archives, churches, cemeteries, and each other via snail mail to piece together the stories of their ancestors. The documents, photos, and records they amassed are humbling and heartbreaking. They tell the stories of Irish and German immigrants who came to America for a better life. They include birth certificates for infants who died days, or mere hours, after being born from things like cholera or diarrhea. US citizenship papers from 1837. An original check ledger from 1880. A hand-sized prayer book given to an ancestor on the day of her first holy communion: June 26, 1898. The original, handwritten suicide note of an unemployed ancestor who killed himself in 1932 by consuming poison while standing on the cemetery lot he owned: "I am very lonesome. Ill mentally and physically. It is time too [sic] go now before I am a public charge." These documents and items serve as tangible supporting evidence for the tales of injustice and ingratitude that Granny and Mommy would revisit over and over again over their tea and Entenmann's crumb cake at the kitchen table.

The grave we're approaching figures prominently in family lore, and I am now the owner of the documents relating to this grave that have been passed down through my ancestors for over a hundred years. The original deed belonged to Margaret Fay, my great-great-grandmother from Ireland. Frederick Faltermann, Sr., husband to Margaret's daughter Hannah (and my mother's grandfather), purchased the plot for Margaret when her husband John died in 1902. There was no gravestone on the site until 1937, when the purchase of "One Barre Granite Monument complete with corner markers" from Fasolino Bros. Memorials for $625 on May 15, 1937 caused an irreparable rift that split one branch of our family tree in two. Apparently, Calvary Cemetery would only allow one surname to appear on each gravestone. My grandfather's side of the family also wanted their last name, Falterman (or Faltermann—I've seen it spelled both ways), on the stone. My mother told me that on the day Hannah, Margaret's daughter, was buried (April 19, 1937), Delia Barry, Margaret's other daughter, "raised a fit" regarding the matter of the stone. She insisted that the Fay name and the Fay name ONLY appear on the stone. Also, I was told that Delia put some sort of restraint on the grave that required members of our family to execute an affidavit before "entering the cemetery" (which I assume means before being buried there). She must have held the deed to the grave at the time because she got her way, even though it's Muriel (aka Daisy, aka Dibby) Falterman, my mother's aunt, whose signature appears on the May 15, 1937 Fasolino Bros. receipt. This conflict between my Irish (Fay) and German (Falterman/n) ancestors was never resolved, and when Granny died sixty-six years later she was still pissed about it.

During my father's gastric bypass surgery, when I asked my mother to tell me some of the most infamous family stories so I could transcribe them onto my computer while we waited in the cafeteria, her final, summarizing remark regarding my Irish, German, and Italian ancestors was this: "The Irish are jealous and vindictive. Germans: concerned with everything being just so. Italians: crazy but loveable."

After Delia died, I think the deed somehow made its way back to our camp, and by that point Calvary had apparently relaxed its rigid aesthetic standards. Over the years Stephen has had all of the names, Fay and Falterman/n alike, added to the gravestone, including the stillborn baby who would have been my mother's big brother; he appears as simply "Baby Faltermann" underneath "Frederick Faltermann," my grandfather— the father and brother my mother never knew.

Stephen's the first one to spot the grave, and he ushers the rest of us over. We gather in a semi-circle around the stone, my father and I standing closest to it on opposite sides. Jack hovers on the periphery, subtly snapping photos. Kenneth and Linda stand beside each other; the children of two of Granny's sisters, they represent the D'Andrea (Italian) faction of the family. Kenneth lays the red roses he brought with him at the base of the gravestone. I pull out the little box containing my mother's ashes. There's no plan, really, for this little ritual, but since I'm the one who organized this gathering, I feel like everyone is looking to me to lead it.

I start talking, though I'm not fully aware of what I'm saying. Words just start spilling out, along with tears. I say something about how my mother and I always had a very complicated relationship. Diana and Deborah nod their heads, as if they understand. I say that regardless of our history together, I knew that she loved me, and I can only hope that she knew I loved her, too. Then the tears and the guilt and the lump in my throat make it hard to give voice to my final thought: I say that when I was growing up, my mother used to tell me how important it had been to her that I have the father and brother she had been denied, and I believe that she wanted this for me because she wanted me to have more love and more opportunities in my life than had been afforded to her. I say that I have always been very grateful to her for that.

My father leans on his cane and cries. He says a few words, but I'm too caught up in my own grief to hear them. Then the others in the circle say their peace. And then I crouch down in front of the gravestone that I have heard about my entire life and empty the contents of a little cardboard box with a label on top that says, "Patricia Blevins."

I stand up and feel the cool breeze across my wet face, the warm sun on the top of my head. I think about Granny. I miss my Granny. I miss my Mommy. I feel like I have failed them both. Logically, rationally, I know this isn't true. But a very young part of me feels like this is all very simple: I was supposed to take care of my mother, but I didn't and she died. My mother was a sad, lonely woman who divorced herself from the world years ago, in part because the world was actively hostile toward her body. She covered herself in spikes as protection. Because those spikes hurt me too, I built my own spikes to protect myself from her. I will never know if she knew how much I loved her, spikes and all.

I hope she is in a place beyond pain. I hope that she has made peace with the body she left behind. I hope that she has made peace with Granny. I hope they're sitting around a kitchen table, drinking tea and eating crumb cake, telling their stories. I hope they can feel my love for them transcending this physical realm in which I am still a body, still a little girl hungry for their love and approval.

When Ray, Daddy, and I recently went through some boxes of my mother's stuff, I found a letter that Granny had written to her dated July 1, 1957. My mother would have been eight years old at the time, and she must have been away at summer camp. At the end of the letter Granny wrote, "today I was thinking about you all day, yesterday too, sweetiepie, see you soon and try not to get any fatter. Love big hugs XXXX Mommy."

"Try not to get any fatter"—my grandmother's instructions to my eight-year-old mother. Six careless words that consumed my mother her entire life. A misguided directive that was passed down to me.

I stand here today as the most well-educated woman in the history of my family, as my mother was before me. I have rights and opportunities that someone like Margaret Fay—an Irish immigrant who gave birth to ten children, lived in a tenement, and couldn't read and write—probably never even imagined. I stand above my dead and feel my heart beat, pumping a hearty cocktail of my immigrant ancestors' blood. I am the literal embodiment of their American dream. And to honor them, to honor my mother, I will honor and love this body. I will use this beautiful mind that my mother gave me and helped to shape. And I will stop wasting so much goddamn time worrying about getting any fatter. Sorry, Granny, but the size of my body does not determine my worth. Fat was never the real enemy, anyway.

As we make our way back to our cars to go to a nearby Italian restaurant for lunch, I watch my father teetering ahead of me with his cane. I worry about him, physically and emotionally. Ever since my mother died, he's been sort of lost. For almost forty-five years they were everything to each other. Losing his partner and best friend so soon after surviving the hell he endured in 2010 was a particularly cruel twist of fate.

All along I had been bracing myself for the death of the wrong parent. Even in death I could not see her. She looked too much like me.

I catch up to the parent who survived and help him to the car.

# Surgery #8, or Back in Black

NORTH CAROLINA, AUGUST 2010

OPERATIVE REPORT

DATE OF SURGERY: 08/04/2010

PROCEDURE PERFORMED: Upper endoscopy. Removal of the stent and debridement of ischial decubitus ulcer with placement of wound vac.

Mr. Blevins is a 61-year-old male well known to the Bariatric service who underwent a previous laparoscopic roux-en-Y gastric bypass complicated by gastrojejunal anastomosic leak. This was subsequently excluded with two covered stents in a series. The patient has done well clinically and it was time to return to the Operating Room for retrieval of the stents. He also had developed a decubitus ulcer in the left ischial area which had some necrotic tissue present on last wound vac change. After discussing the risks, benefits and alternatives, the patient and his family elected to proceed with the recommended procedure.

. . . After removal of the stents, the gastric pouch was evaluated in healthy condition with pink mucosa and no evidence of any perforation and good insufflation maintained, again consistent with resolution of this leak . . .

It took five months to fix my father's leak, and close to four months to fix the leak in the Gulf of Mexico. On August 3, 2010, BP successfully performed a "static kill" of the Macondo well, effectively ending the flow of oil out of the well by pumping in dense drilling mud. On August 4, 2010, Dr. Belfore removed my father's stents and determined that his leak had been "resolved."

However, neither disaster was really over, of course. The water, wildlife, and economy in the Gulf had been utterly ravaged, and the consequences of the spill will likely persist for decades. As a result of his gastric bypass experience, my father left the ICU with stage 2 kidney disease, a heart condition, a stage 4 decubitus that would require reconstructive surgery and another lengthy hospital stay, a ventilator-dependency that would take months to kick, and a deconditioned body that would necessitate many more months of physical therapy to strengthen. But, he did leave it.

On the morning of August 19, I got to the ICU early to help prep my father for his transfer to a long-term care facility in Greensboro (the dirty, depressing one I had toured in late June ended up being the only viable option). When I got there, the nurses had just finished removing my father's rectal tube. He handed me the dry-erase board when I approached the bed. It read, "Having an anal catheter removed is like giving birth to a fawn." I laughed as he nodded emphatically.

For the second time, I rode in the ambulance with him. This time we were in a fancy, luxury ambulance specifically designed for transporting critically ill patients. I climbed in the front passenger seat as they loaded him into the back. "Hey, Daddy—I'm up here," I said. He gave me a thumbs-up. As we pulled out of the ambulance bay, AC/DC's "Back in Black" started playing on the radio. I asked the driver to turn it up.

Then we got on I-40, heading west.

# Epilogue: Limited by Body Habitus

MEDICAL RECORDS, MARCH–DECEMBER 2010

Mr. Blevins is a 61 [year] old male who reports a long history of obesity.

> Mr. Blevins is a 61-year-old male who is my father.

He is an unfortunate 61-year-old gentleman who had a Roux-en-Y weight loss reduction surgery on March 24th and presented now, first to ———————— County and now to here in septic shock.

> He is an unfortunate 61-year-old gentleman who is now foaming at the mouth.

This is a morbidly obese gentleman lying in bed comfortable, intubated and sedated.

> *fat*

61-year-old obese male with acute renal failure. Due to the patient's obesity, the femoral access sites will likely not provide good dialysis.

> *overweight, obese, morbidly obese*

Large patient body habitus limit the examination.

> *underheight, obeast, ginormous*

Patient body habitus limits detail.

> *generously proportioned, gravitationally challenged, fluffy*

There is limitation due to body habitus.

> *roly-poly, jelly-belly, pot-bellied*

ABD: very obese
Ext: obese
He is malnourished

*pig, sow, heifer, cow*

The PICC line is poorly visualized secondary to the patient's
very large body habitus and the portable technique.

*lazy, lazy asshole, fat bitch, fat asshole, fat-ass, lard-ass, fat-so,*
*fatty, fatty-fatty-two-by-four-can't-get-through-the-kitchen-door*

Exam limited by patient obesity and portable technique.

*fat*


Respiratory failure requiring mechanical ventilation.

I watch a machine breathe for my father,

ventilated, eyes open

and I think about love.

This study is limited by patient body habitus.

Tangible, four-dimensional memories of love:

The film is limited by body habitus.

big arms wrapped around little bodies,

Abd: obese, drainage tubes R abdomen

delicious food prepared by stable people,

## EPILOGUE

Radiographic evaluation is limited by patient's morbid obesity
and the portable technique.

> the sweaty forehead of my sleeping brother,

Study is somewhat limited due to patient's large body habitus
and portable technique.

> crying in my mother's lap without shame.

Study limited [due] to patient's body habitus and inability to
cooperate with the exam.

> I wear an iron gown,
> pour barium down my father's throat,
> and think about the inconvenience of love:

thinks he is in south korea

> sacrifices made by the old for their clueless young,

answers "yes" to all questions

> the blind devotion of the young for their fallible old.

Daughter @ bedside. Pt responsive to daughter.

> The thoughts roll through my head like grenades,

Abdomen: Obese

> each one exploding when it reaches the center.

We will perform an open removal of remnant stomach.

> He which hath no stomach to this fight,

The stomach was freed and was passed posteriorly to the Roux
limb and pulled over to the right side of the abdomen.

> Let him depart; his passport shall be made
> And crowns for convoy put into his purse:

ESTIMATED BLOOD LOSS: 2200mL

> We would not die in that man's company
> That fears his fellowship to die with us.

The patient is a pleasant, obese, but somewhat lethargic
sedated white male who is bedridden in no acute distress.

> Wake up, Daddy.

Neck obese, 0 scars. Supple.

> We have to get the ring to Mordor.

The patient is a morbidly obese 61-year-old male who had a
Roux-en-Y gastric bypass several months ago. He had multiple
complications and has chronic respiratory failure, and I have
been asked to perform a tracheostomy.

> Beware the Jabberwock, my son!

Ventilator dependent.

> The jaws that bite, the claws that catch!

The heart is enlarged.

> In the fell clutch of circumstance

The heart appears to be at upper limits of normal for size.

> I have not winced nor cried aloud.

# EPILOGUE

The patient is obese making evaluation more difficult.

> Under the bludgeonings of chance

Difficult vent wean [due to] deconditioning, body habitus and severe anxiety.

> My head is bloody, but unbowed.

The patient is a pleasant obese man lying in bed in no acute distress.
He weighed 359 preop and now weighs 237.
He is a pleasant, mildly obese man with very poor muscle tone.
An obese white male in no distress.
He has not been out of bed since March. He has been depressed.

Since his second hospitalization
since a small leak would be difficult to exclude
since his abdomen was too hostile
Since his gastric bypass he has lost over 100 pounds.

exquisitely rare

> Indeed.

Mr. Blevins is a 61-year-old man with an exquisitely complicated past medical history.

> Mr. Blevins is my father.

Mr. Blevins is a 61-year-old male well known to the Bariatric service

> Mr. Blevins is an impenetrable box.

Mr. Blevins is a 61-year-old pleasant Caucasian male

> I've never died in this world before.

Mr. Blevins' hospital course was otherwise uneventful

> How do I get from my world to your world?

Mr. Blevins eventually did alright and was discharged from the hospital.

> Do I owe anybody anything?

All the patient's and his daughter's questions were answered.

> I promise I'll make this up to you.

Thank you very much for allowing us to participate in the care of this pleasant gentleman.

> (dream diamond mine, dream basement)

Thank you for the opportunity to contribute to the care of your patient.

> We are all limited by body habitus.

Thank you very much for allowing me to see James Blevins.

# Notes

The excerpts of my father's medical records that appear throughout this book were used with his express consent. I have removed the names of all individuals other than my father, as well as the names of the hospitals that treated him. The only other name that appears (Dr. Belfore) has been changed.

## Preface

ix    *According to a 2011 study, some Americans would rather be blind, lose a limb, or give up five years of their lives than be obese*: Alexandra A. Brewis, Daniel J. Hruschka & Amber Wutich, "Vulnerability to Fat-Stigma in Women's Everyday Relationships," *Social Science & Medicine* 73 (2011): 491-497, 494.

## When Diet and Exercise Just Aren't Enough

6    The title for this chapter comes from the recording that would play on the hospital phone system when I called the ICU front desk from the waiting room to ask permission to enter and would be placed on hold. One of the commercials that I was forced to listen to repeatedly that year advertised the hospital's weight-loss surgery program, for "when diet and exercise just aren't enough."

6    *Gastric bypass, or Roux-en-Y, is currently considered the "gold standard" of surgical weight-loss procedures*: "Bariatric Surgery Procedures," American Society for Metabolic and Bariatric Surgery, accessed February 22, 2019, https://asmbs.org/patients/bariatric-surgery-procedures.

6    *When successful, it is generally believed that gastric bypass serves as an impressive example of the medical industry's ability to cure the "disease" of obesity*: "Benefits of Bariatric Surgery," American Society for Metabolic and Bariatric Surgery, accessed February 28, 2019, https://asmbs.org/patients/benefits-of-bariatric-surgery.

6    *When unsuccessful, gastric bypass can cause internal bleeding, bowel obstruction, infection, pulmonary embolism, and death*: "Gastric Bypass Surgery: Risks," Mayo Foundation for Medical Education and Research (MFMER), accessed February 28, 2019, http://www.mayoclinic.org/tests-procedures/bariatric-surgery/basics/risks/prc-20019138.

6    *"a public health issue that is among the most burdensome faced by the Nation"*: "The Surgeon General's Call to Action to Prevent and Decrease Overweight and Obesity," Office of the Surgeon General (US); Office of Disease Prevention and Health Promotion (US); Centers for Disease Control and Prevention (US); National Institutes of Health (US). Rockville (MD): Office of the Surgeon General (US), 2001, accessed February 28, 2019, https://www.ncbi.nlm.nih.gov/books/NBK44210/.

6    *the American Medical Association, Medicaid, and Medicare currently classify obesity as a disease*: Andrew Pollack, "A.M.A. Recognizes Obesity as a Disease," *New York Times*, June 18, 2013, http://www.nytimes.com/2013/06/19/business/ama-recognizes-obesity-as-a-disease.html?_r=0.

7    *BMI as a poor indicator of health*: A. J. Tomiyama, J. M. Hunger, J. Nguyen-Cuu & C. Wells, "Misclassification of cardiometabolic health when using body mass index categories in NHANES 2005–2012," *International Journal of Obesity* 40, no. 5 (2016): 883-886.

7    *In 1998, the National Institutes of Health lowered BMI levels*: Sally Squires, "Optimal Weight Threshold Lowered," *Washington Post*, June 4, 1998, http://www.washingtonpost.com/wp-srv/style/guideposts/fitness/optimal.htm.

7    *The International Obesity Task Force…had direct financial ties to pharmaceutical companies that manufactured diet pills for profit*: Ray Moynihan, "Obesity task force linked to WHO takes 'millions' from drug firms," *BMJ*, June 17, 2006, https://www.ncbi.nlm.nih.gov/pmc/articles/PMC1479667/.

7    *Currently, approximately 228,000 weight loss surgeries are performed each year in the US*: "Estimate of Bariatric Surgery Numbers, 2011-2017," American Society for Metabolic and Bariatric Surgery, accessed February 22, 2019, https://asmbs.org/resources/estimate-of-bariatric-surgery-numbers.

7    *at a cost of $15,000 – $25,000 per surgery*: "Definition & Facts for Bariatric Surgery," National Institute of Diabetes and Digestive and Kidney Diseases, accessed February 22, 2019, https://www.niddk.nih.gov/health-information/weight-management/bariatric-surgery/definition-facts.

7    *In 2018, the total value of the US weight loss market was $72 billion*: John LaRosa, "Top 9 Things to Know About the Weight Loss Industry," *Market Research Blog*, accessed March 6, 2019, https://blog.marketresearch.com/u.s.-weight-loss-industry-grows-to-72-billion.

## We Tell Ourselves Stories in Order to Live

8    The title of this chapter comes from Joan Didion's *We Tell Ourselves Stories in Order to Live: Collected Nonfiction* (New York: Alfred A. Knopf, 2006).

## A Note Regarding Writing About My Mother

13    *"both an attack on her mother and an expression of love for her"*: Nancy J. Chodorow, *The Reproduction of Mothering: Psychoanalysis and the Sociology of Gender* (Berkley: University of California Press, 1999), 126.

## I Would Not Recommend My Program

22    *"a medically-supervised weight-management program"*: "About the Optifast Program," accessed February 28, 2019, https://www.optifast.com/about-optifastr-program.

23    *"Fat isn't always bad. And exercise isn't always good"*: Carl J. Lavie, M.D., *The Obesity Paradox: When Thinner Means Sicker and Heavier Means Healthier* (New York: Penguin, 2014), x.

23    *Lavie (and other physicians) have identified a "paradox" in regards to obesity*: I feel I should note that Lavie has been criticized for accepting research funding from Coca-Cola. (Julia Belluz, "The Obesity Paradox: Why Coke is Promoting a Theory That Being Fat Won't Hurt Your Health," *Vox*, October 20, 2015.) Lavie claims that Coke has only funded a few of his lectures. (Olga Khazan, "Why Scientists Can't Agree on Whether It's Unhealthy to be Overweight," *Atlantic*, August 14, 2017.) Since I am not a physician or scientist, I am not equipped to speak to the validity of Lavie's study, or to that of any of the studies that I mention in this book. I simply offer them as different viewpoints to consider.

24    *"Low fitness, smoking, high blood pressure, low income and loneliness are all better predictors of early death than obesity"*: Sandra Aamodt, *Why Diets Make Us Fat: The Unintended Consequences of Our Obsession with Weight Loss* (Brunswick: Scribe, 2016), 22.

24    *"The benefits of dieting are simply too small and the potential harms of dieting are too large for it to be recommended as a safe and effective treatment for obesity"*: Traci Mann, et al., "Medicare's Search for Effective Obesity Treatments: Diets Are Not the Answer," *American Psychologist* 62, no. 3 (2007): 220-233, 230. See also: A. Janet Tomiyama, Britt Ahlstrom & Traci Mann, "Long-Term Effects of Dieting: Is Weight Loss Related to Health?" *Social and Personality Psychology Compass* 7, no. 12 (2013): 861-877.

24    *A 2016 study of former* The Biggest Loser *contestants*: Erin Fothergill, et al., "Persistent Metabolic Adaptation 6 Years After 'The Biggest Loser' Competition," *Obesity* 24, no. 8 (2016): 1612-1619.

24    *a study that suggests our weight is at least partially determined by our bodies' ability to process carbon dioxide*: Philip D. Welsby, "Why Diets Fail: A Hypothesis for Discussion," *Postgrad Med J* (2016): 1-4. Welsby writes, "Unless there are changes in ventilatory carbon excretion, 'metabolism,' 'genetic factors,' 'hormones' or 'exercise' do not provide complete explanatory mechanisms for weight changes, obesity and failure of diets. Low sensitivity

of respiratory centres to carbon dioxide may cause overweight and dietary failures after initial weight loss" (1). He concludes that doctors "should cease teaching that weight regulation depends exclusively on calorie dynamics" (3).

## He Which Hath No Stomach to This Fight

55    *"Out of the night that covers me"*: William Ernest Henley, "Invictus," accessed June 3, 2019, https://www.poetryfoundation.org/poems/51642/invictus.

56    *"'Twas brillig, and the slithy toves"*: Lewis Carroll, "Jabberwocky," accessed September 4, 2018, https://www.poetryfoundation.org/poems/42916/jabberwocky.

57    *"If we are mark'd to die, we are enow"*: William Shakespeare, *Henry V*, Act IV, Scene III, accessed September 4, 2018, http://shakespeare.mit.edu/henryv/henryv.4.3.html.

## Medical Records Medley

74    *if you are unable to perform your job because of the size of his "body habitus" and the "portable technique," then perhaps you should develop a new technique. And get better at your fucking job*: A 2006 study published in the scientific journal *Radiology* traces the increase of the use of the phrase "limited due to body habitus" in radiology reports between 1989 and 2003 (Raul N. Uppot, et al., "Effect of Obesity on Image Quality: Fifteen-year Longitudinal Study for Evaluation of Dictated Radiology Reports," *Radiology* 240, no. 2 [2006]: 435-439). In the press release about the study, Dr. Uppot, the lead researcher, is quoted as saying, "Americans need to know that obesity can hinder their medical care when they enter a hospital," which implies that he believes the problem is the patients' fault (Radiological Society of North America, "Obesity an Increasing Obstacle to Medical Diagnosis," press release, July 25, 2006, https://press.rsna.org/timssnet/media/pressreleases/pr_target.cfm?ID=284). Thankfully, an editorial in *Academic Radiology* published eight years later urges radiologists to "closely evaluate the diagnostic performance/comparative effectiveness of imaging technologies in the context of varying body habitus," perhaps indicating a shift in the way radiologists view fat bodies (Chamith S. Rajapakse & Gregory Chang, "Impact of Body Habitus on Radiologic Interpretations," *Academic Radiology* 21, no. 1 [2014]: 1-2).

## Not Quite Human

76    *"inherent connections to fundamental beliefs about race, class, and the evolutionary 'fitness' for citizenship"*: Amy Erdman Farrell, *Fat Shame: Stigma and the Fat Body in American Culture* (New York: New York University Press, 2011), 115.

76    *"fat people are often treated as not quite human, entities to whom the normal standards of polite and respectful behavior do not seem to apply"*: Farrell, *Fat Shame*, 6.

77    *some argue that the "war on fat" is also an attempt to delineate symbolic boundaries between populations based on race and socio-economic status*: See April Michelle Herndon, "Collateral Damage From Friendly Fire?: Race, Nation, and Class and the 'War Against Obesity,'" *Social Semiotics* 15, no. 2 (2005): 127-141; Robert L. Reece, "Coloring Weight Stigma: On Race, Colorism, Weight Stigma, and the Failure of Additive Intersectionality," *Sociology of Race and Ethnicity* (2018): 1-13; and Sabrina Strings, *Fearing the Black Body: The Racial Origins of Fat Phobia* (New York: New York University Press, 2019).

77    *"this cultural conflict got played out—and continues to get played out—on the body"*: Farrell, *Fat Shame*, 44.

77    *The anonymous comments that followed a 2012 article*: JoNel Aleccia, "Donating Your Body to Science? Nobody Wants a Chubby Corpse," NBC News, January 9, 2012, http://www.nbcnews.com/health/health-news/donating-your-body-science-nobody-wants-chubby-corpse-f1C6436539. The comments I reference have been removed from the website since I first accessed the article in May 2012.

## Deepwater Horizon

87    *"By the time the rig crew acted"*: *Deep Water: The Gulf Oil Disaster and the Future of Offshore Drilling*. Report to the President: National Commission on the BP Deepwater Horizon Oil Spill and Offshore Drilling, January 2011, https://www.govinfo.gov/app/details/GPO-OILCOMMISSION.

## Another Leak

88    *On April 20, 2010, the Deepwater Horizon oil rig exploded*: In my research on the oil spill, I relied primarily on the following sources: Antonia Juhasz, *Black Tide: The Devastating Impact of the Gulf Oil Spill* (New Jersey: John Wiley & Sons, Inc., 2011); John Konrad & Tom Shroder, *Fire on the Horizon: The Untold Story of the Gulf Oil Disaster* (New York: Harper Collins, 2011); Bob Cavnar, *Disaster on the Horizon: High Stakes, High Risks, and the Story Behind the Deepwater Well Blowout* (White River Junction, Vermont: Chelsea Green Publishing, 2010); Joel Achenbach, *A Hole at the Bottom of the Sea: The Race to Kill the BP Oil Gusher* (New York: Simon & Schuster, 2011); David Barstow, David Rohde & Stephanie Saul, "Deepwater Horizon's Final Hours," *New York Times*, December 25, 2010; and "BP Oil Spill Timeline," *Guardian*, July 22, 2010. I am grateful to Antonia Juhasz for speaking with me over the phone about her experience of writing *Black Tide*.

88    *the "rig [that] set the standard for all the others"*: Achenbach, *A Hole at the Bottom of the Sea*, 14.

88    *Some oil industry experts have compared drilling wells in 5,000 to 10,000 feet of water to*

*performing surgery at the bottom of the ocean*: In *Disaster on the Horizon*, Bob Cavnar writes, "Drilling wells in 5,000 to 10,000 feet of water has been likened to working on the surface of the moon or heart surgery at the bottom of the ocean" (33). Lamar McKay, BP America chairman and president during the disaster, told ABC that repairing the leak was "like doing open heart surgery at 5,000 feet (1,524 metres) in the dark with robot-controlled submarines." "US Oil Spill Plug like 'Open-Heart Surgery' in the Dark," *Sydney Morning Herald*, May 3, 2010, https://www.smh.com.au/environment/us-oil-spill-plug-like-openheart-surgery-in-the-dark-bp-20100503-u21a.html.

89    *"Because this leak is unique and unprecedented, it could take many days to stop"*: "President Barack Obama: Gulf Oil Spill Could Jeopardize the Livelihoods of Thousands of Americans," *Times-Picayune*, May 2, 2010, http://www.nola.com/news/gulf-oil-spill/index.ssf/2010/05/transcript_of_president_barack.html.

## Surely They All Knew What They Were Doing, Didn't They?

93    *"At this time there is no crude emanating from that wellhead at the ocean floor"*: Juhasz, *Black Tide*, 63.

93    *"If it contained good news, it wasn't true"*: Achenbach, *A Hole at the Bottom of the Sea*, 79.

94    *"Surely they all knew what they were doing, didn't they?"*: Juhasz, *Black Tide*, 234.

94    *"Mother Nature just doesn't want to be drilled here"*: Achenbach, *A Hole at the Bottom of the Sea*, 15.

## I Would Like My Life Back

106   *"There's no one who wants this over more than I do. I would like my life back"*: "BP Chief to Gulf Residents: 'I'm Sorry,'" CNN, May 30, 2010, http://www.cnn.com/2010/US/05/30/gulf.oil.spill/index.html.

## Just Like a Crime Scene

108   *From a BP press release*: "Update on Gulf of Mexico oil spill - 29 May," BP press release, May 28, 2010, https://www.bp.com/en/global/corporate/news-and-insights/press-releases/update-on-gulf-of-mexico-oil-spill-29-may.html.

109   *"financial self-dealing, accepting gifts from energy companies, cocaine use and sexual misconduct"*: Charlie Savage, "Sex, Drug Use and Graft Cited in Interior Department," *New York Times*, September 10, 2008, https://www.nytimes.com/2008/09/11/washington/11royalty.html.

109   *offshore drilling leases are the second largest source of income for the US Treasury*: "Will

revenue sharing spur more offshore drilling?," Global Energy Institute, US Chamber of Commerce, accessed September 4, 2018, https://www.globalenergyinstitute.org/will-revenue-sharing-spur-more-offshore-drilling.

109 *"I realized that it was just like a crime scene…They killed our Gulf, and now the murderer is in charge of cleaning up the scene of the crime"*: Juhasz, *Black Tide*, 198.

## I See Fat People

136 *Studies have shown that many medical practitioners are biased against fat patients*: See Sean M. Phelan, et al., "Impact of Weight Bias and Stigma on Quality of Care and Outcomes for Patients with Obesity," *Obesity Reviews* 16, no. 4 (2015): 319-326; Sean M. Phelan, et al., "Implicit and Explicit Weight Bias in a National Sample of 4,732 Medical Students: The Medical Student CHANGES Study," *Obesity* 22, no. 4 (2014): 1201-1208; Gary D. Foster, et al., "Primary Care Physicians' Attitudes about Obesity and its Treatment," *Obesity* 11, no. 10 (2003): 1168-1177; and Marlene B. Schwartz, et al., "Weight Bias Among Health Professionals Specializing in Obesity," *Obesity* 11, no. 9 (2003): 1033-1039.

136 *"viewed obese patients as awkward, unattractive, ugly, and noncompliant"*: Foster, et al., "Primary Care Physicians' Attitudes about Obesity and its Treatment," 1168.

137 *"more negative toward obese people than toward racial minorities, gays, lesbians, and poor people"*: Phelan, et al., "Implicit and Explicit Weight Bias in a National Sample of 4,732 Medical Students," 1201.

137 *the "obesity specialists" in their study "associated the stereotypes lazy, stupid, and worthless with obese people"*: Schwartz, et al., "Weight Bias Among Health Professionals Specializing in Obesity," 1037.

137 *"Fat presents an* apparent *paradox because it is visible and dissected publicly; in this respect, it is* hypervisible. *Fat is also marginalized and erased; in this respect, it is* hyperinvisible*"*: Jeannine A. Gailey, *The Hyper(in)visible Fat Woman: Weight and Gender Discourse in Contemporary Society* (New York: Palgrave Macmillan, 2014), 7.

## Full Disclosure

141 *"why we were gaining so much weight and what we could do to stop it"*: J. Eric Oliver, *Fat Politics: The Real Story Behind America's Obesity Epidemic* (New York: Oxford University Press, 2006), 2.

141 *"began to look a lot more like a politically orchestrated campaign to capitalize on America's growing weight"*: Oliver, *Fat Politics*, x.

141 *such as attributing the deaths of* all *obese people to their fat, even if they had died from a snakebite or a car crash*: The two studies that commenced the "war on obesity" are D.

Allison, et al., "Annual Deaths Attributable to Obesity in the United States," *Journal of the American Medical Association* 282 (1999): 1530-1538 and A. Mokdad, et al., "Actual Causes of Death in the United States, 2000," *Journal of the American Medical Association* 291 (2004): 1238-1245. Oliver notes that "in neither of these studies did the researchers actually measure the linkage between obesity and death" (24).

142   *the BMI chart was created by a Belgian astronomer in the 1830s*: Adolphe Quetelet devised the BMI scale as a tool for determining whether the laws of probability used in astronomy could also be applied to humans. BMI, therefore, was developed as a method for classifying individuals and identifying an "average" size, which Quetelet decided was the "ideal." The insurance industry adopted his scale in the 1940s and 50s (and used it as justification for charging fat people higher premiums), and the government and medical community followed suit shortly thereafter. Oliver writes, "Ultimately, the most influential factor in determining what Americans considered to be overweight was not based on criteria of health but criteria of profit and measurement within the insurance industry" (19).

142   *"[c]oncern about weight and dieting is not timeless; its origins are modern and can be quite precisely traced"*: Peter N. Stearns, *Fat History: Bodies and Beauty in the Modern West* (New York: New York University Press, 1997), xx.

142   *"much of the causation of the growing medical concern about weight came from patient pressure, rather than the other way around"*: Stearns, *Fat History*, 45.

143   *"Weight is a cultural condition"*: Hillel Schwartz, *Never Satisfied: A Cultural History of Diets, Fantasies and Fat* (New York: Macmillan, 1986), 4.

143   *the word "diet" didn't obtain its modern meaning until 1910*: Stearns, *Fat History*, 8.

# Acknowledgments

ONE OF THE most valuable life lessons my mother taught me was the importance of expressing gratitude. She used to have me sit at the kitchen table and handwrite thank-you notes for people who had given me presents, often making me go through multiple drafts before she was satisfied. I hated the ritual as a child, but it has become a sacred act to me as an adult. Which is why I have spent the last nine years being deeply bothered by the fact that I never properly thanked all of the many kind individuals who helped me survive 2010. Some sent gifts to cheer me up or money to help pay for my plane tickets, others showed up at the hospital with food or took me out for meals, and a few dropped everything they were doing to show up for me when I needed them. If you are one of the people who helped me that year, I am sorry if I never properly thanked you. Please know that your generosity saved me, as it was a source of light and hope during a very dark and difficult time. I am perpetually grateful for your kindness.

I am also grateful for the many excellent medical practitioners who took care of my father. Thank you for putting up with the drama, pain, shit, piss, heartache, tedium, and angst of my father's medical disaster. I can only pray that on the worst day of my life, when I feel all hope is lost, I look up from a hospital bed and see one of you standing above me, urging me to breathe.

My years in graduate school and the wonderful teachers and fellow students I met during my journey were pivotal in helping me write and develop this book. I am indebted to the English departments of Wake Forest University and the University of South Carolina for serving as academic incubators for this project. In particular, I wish to thank the following individuals for directly or indirectly helping me birth this book: Eric G. Wilson, Mary K. DeShazer, Catherine Keyser, James Barilla, Nikky Finney, Laura Jennings, Jessica Handler, Ed Madden, Debra Rae Cohen, Federica Clementi, and my MFA cohort at USC.

I might have never made it to graduate school—or even discovered that I was a writer—if it had not been for my involvement with the actors and writers of Visible Theatre in New York City from 2005-2010. I am indebted to Kala Smith and Michael Quattrone (who now run Hearthfire), as well as the many other brilliant and brave artists I encountered through Visible Theatre, for giving me the courage to start this journey, and for helping me find my voice.

When I started working on this project, I knew nothing about the fat acceptance movement or the field of Fat Studies. I am grateful to the community I have found through my involvement with the Fat Studies area of the Popular Culture Association national conferences for teaching me about fat activism, body acceptance, and the importance of considering other points of view.

I am incredibly thankful that *Limited By Body Habitus* found a home with Autumn House Press. Many thanks to Christine Stroud and Shelby Newsom for their editorial support, and to guest judge Daisy Hernández for choosing my book.

As aforementioned, the kindness and generosity of many people helped me get through the events that I depict in this book. Gail Pierpoint, thank you for taking me in and treating me as if I were your own. Jackson Katz and Kristin Cunliffe, thank you for loving me and showing up on my darkest days. Dr. Stacy Wentworth, thank you for your unwavering friendship and invaluable medical advice. Russell Roten, thank you for your sound counsel. Jennifer Hill, thank you for providing me with a place of solace. Finally, I am beholden to the following friends for their various acts of kindness during my father's medical disaster: Tim and Thelma Bryson, Ginny and Ben Marks, Karen Horne Beasley, Ariane Reinhart, Kyle Covington, Moni Hendrix, Dasha Snyder, Sonora Chase, Brian and Cindy Yandle, Dana Lancaster, Cher Lair, K. Leigh Hamm Forell, and D. B.

I am grateful to my partner Lance Hall for his inexorable optimism and steadfast love; thank you for being my favorite reader. Also, many thanks to Lucy and Ian Hall for inviting me into their home and their lives; watching you grow is both a privilege and a joy.

To my brother, Ray Blevins: Thank you for continuing to battle your demons. I still love you the most.

To my father, Jim Blevins: Thank you for your courage, perseverance, and indomitable wit. I appreciate your sacrifices, and I am honored to be your valkyrie.

Finally, I am eternally grateful to Marie Clark Blevins, Helen D'Andrea Faltermann, and Patricia Faltermann Blevins for supporting me, challenging me, and believing in me. I wish you could read this book. I wish you were alive to see the strong woman you created thrive.

# New and Forthcoming Releases

*Cage of Lit Glass* by Charles Kell ❀ Winner of the 2018 Autumn House Poetry Prize, selected by Kimiko Hahn

*Not Dead Yet and Other Stories* by Hadley Moore ❀ Winner of the 2018 Autumn House Fiction Prize, selected by Dana Johnson

*Limited by Body Habitus: An American Fat Story* by Jennifer Renee Blevins ❀ Winner of the 2018 Autumn House Nonfiction Prize, selected by Daisy Hernández

*Belief Is Its Own Kind of Truth, Maybe* by Lori Jakiela

*Epithalamia* by Erinn Batykefer ❀ Winner of the 2018 Autumn House Chapbook Prize, selected by Gerry LaFemina

*Praise Song for My Children: New and Selected Poems* by Patricia Jabbeh Wesley

*Heartland Calamitous* by Michael Credico

*Voice Message* by Katherine Barrett Swett ❀ Winner of the 2019 Donald Justice Poetry Prize, selected by Erica Dawson

*The Gutter Spread Guide to Prayer* by Eric Tran ❀ Winner of the 2019 Rising Writer Prize, selected by Stacey Waite

For our full catalog please visit: autumnhouse.org